Let's give our children lots of love and care so that they have a healthy and happy childhood.

Charlie Design Production©

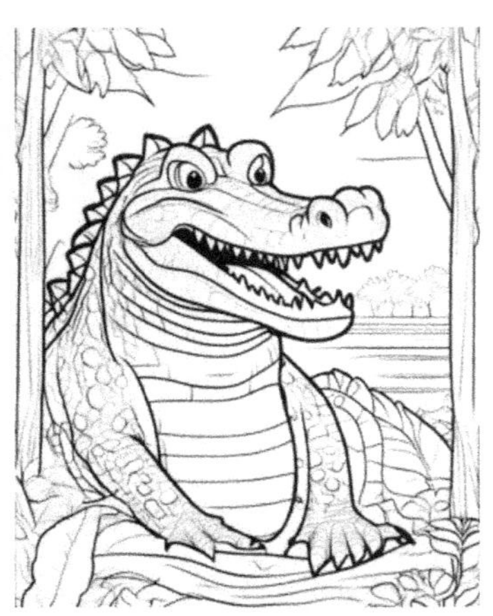
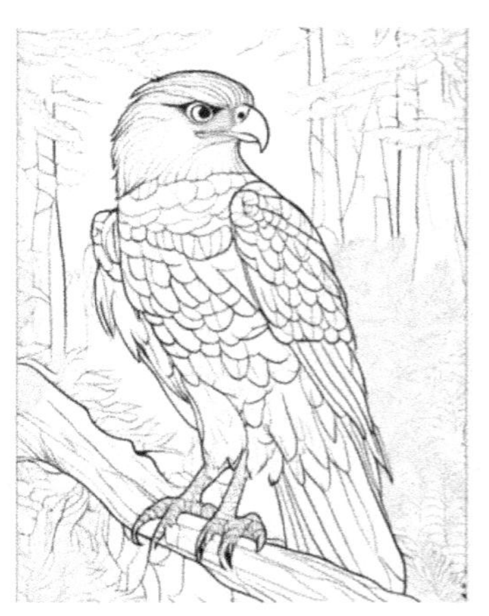
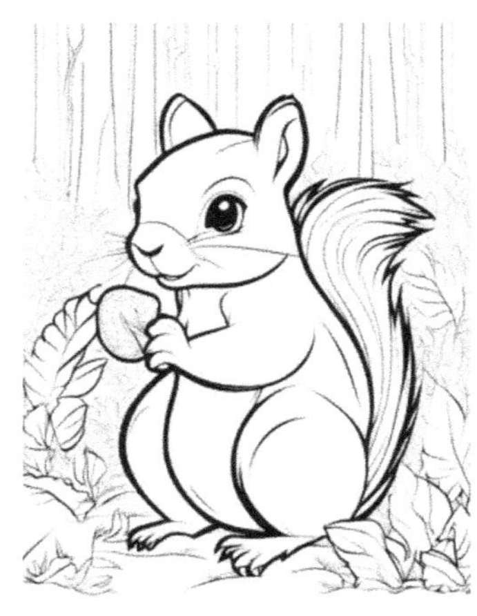

This Book Belongs to:

____

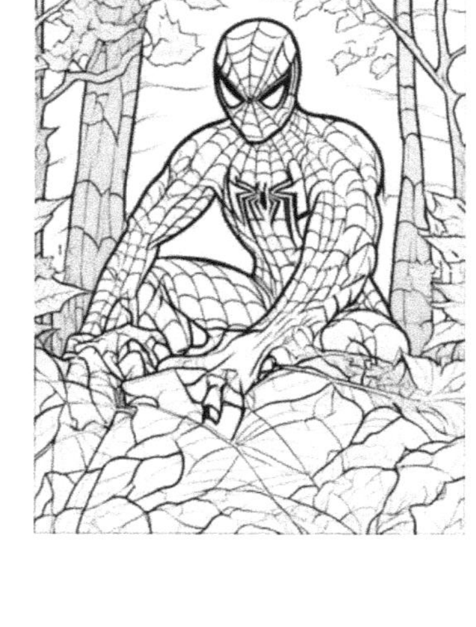

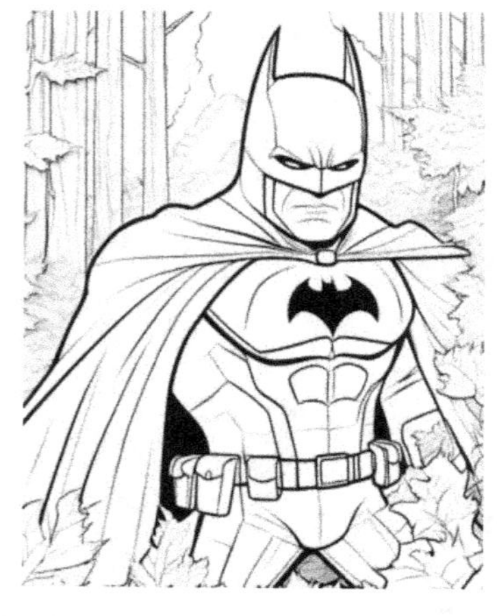
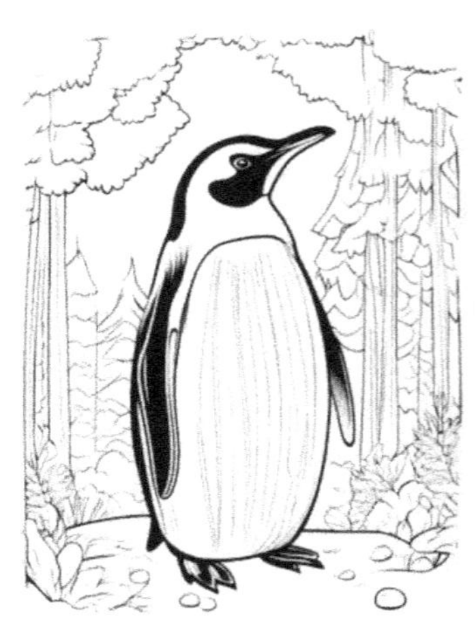

Charlie Design Production ©

Test Color Page

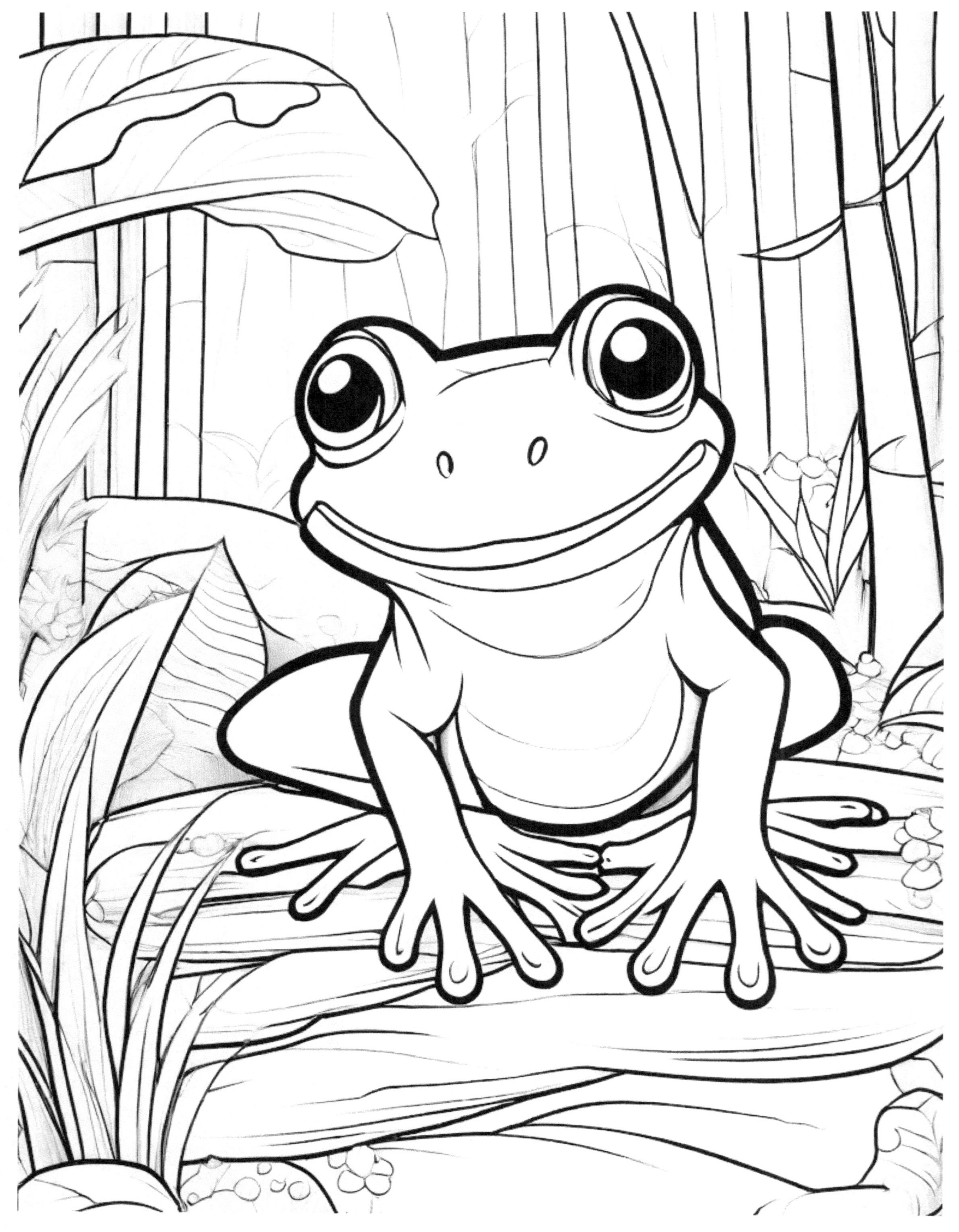

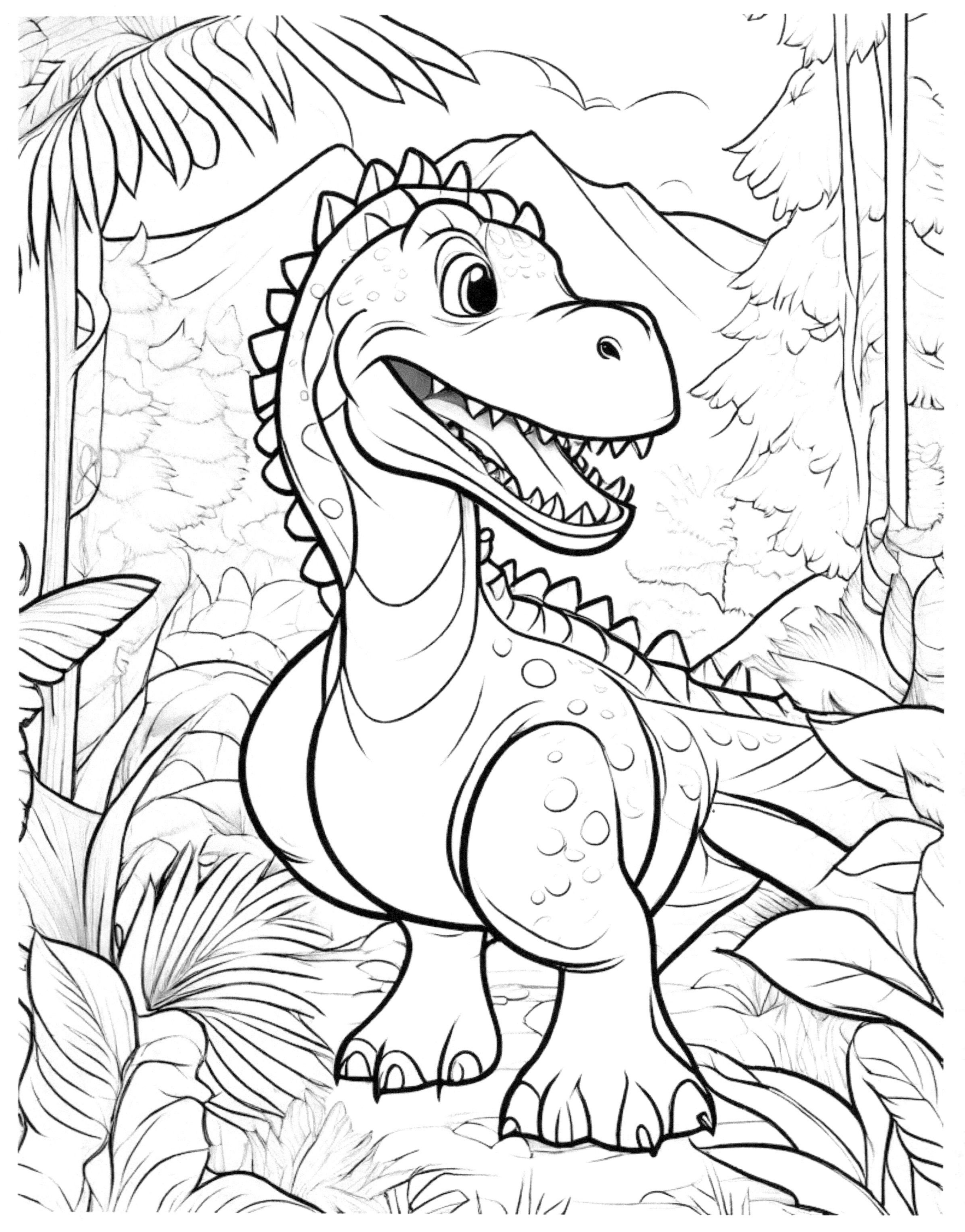

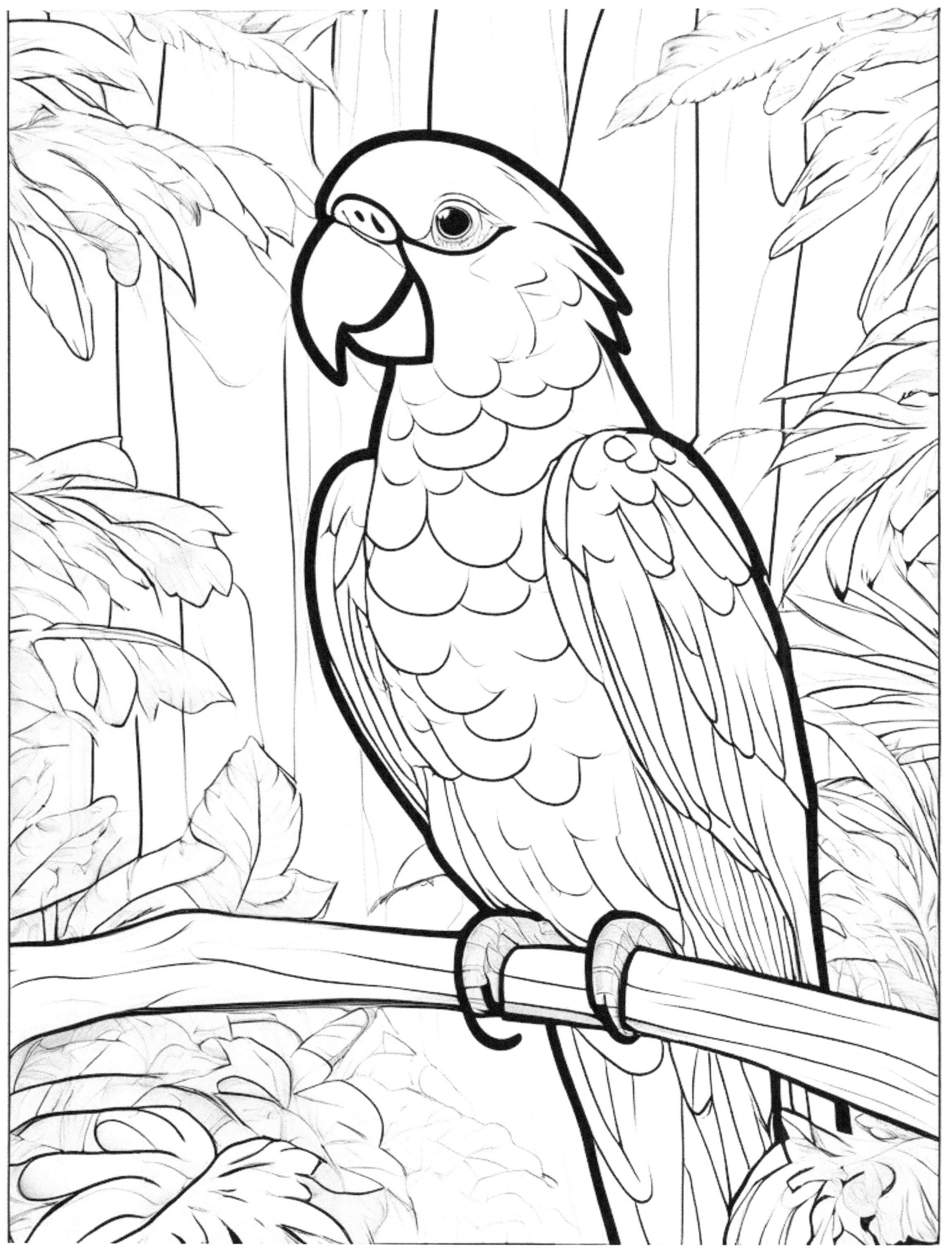

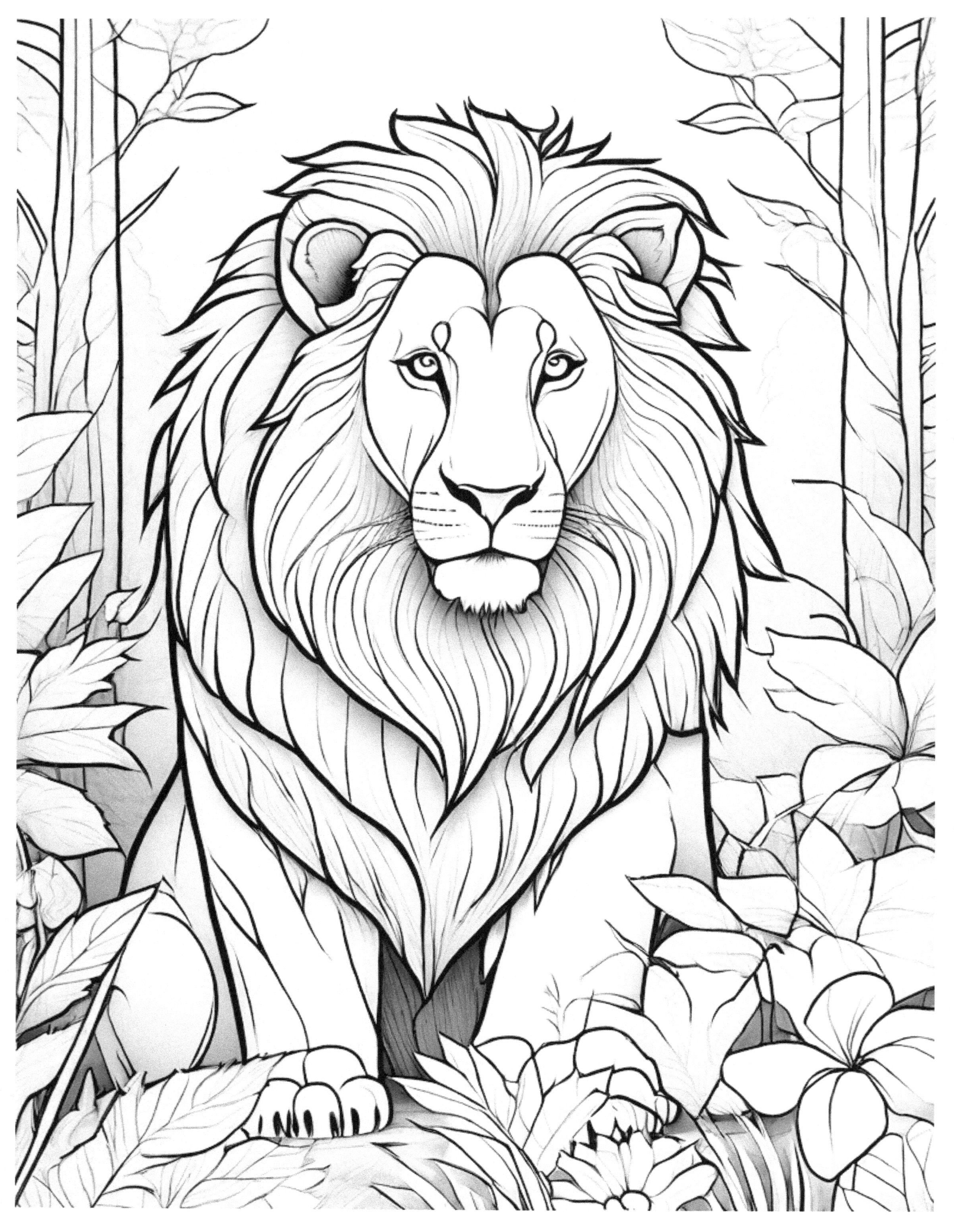

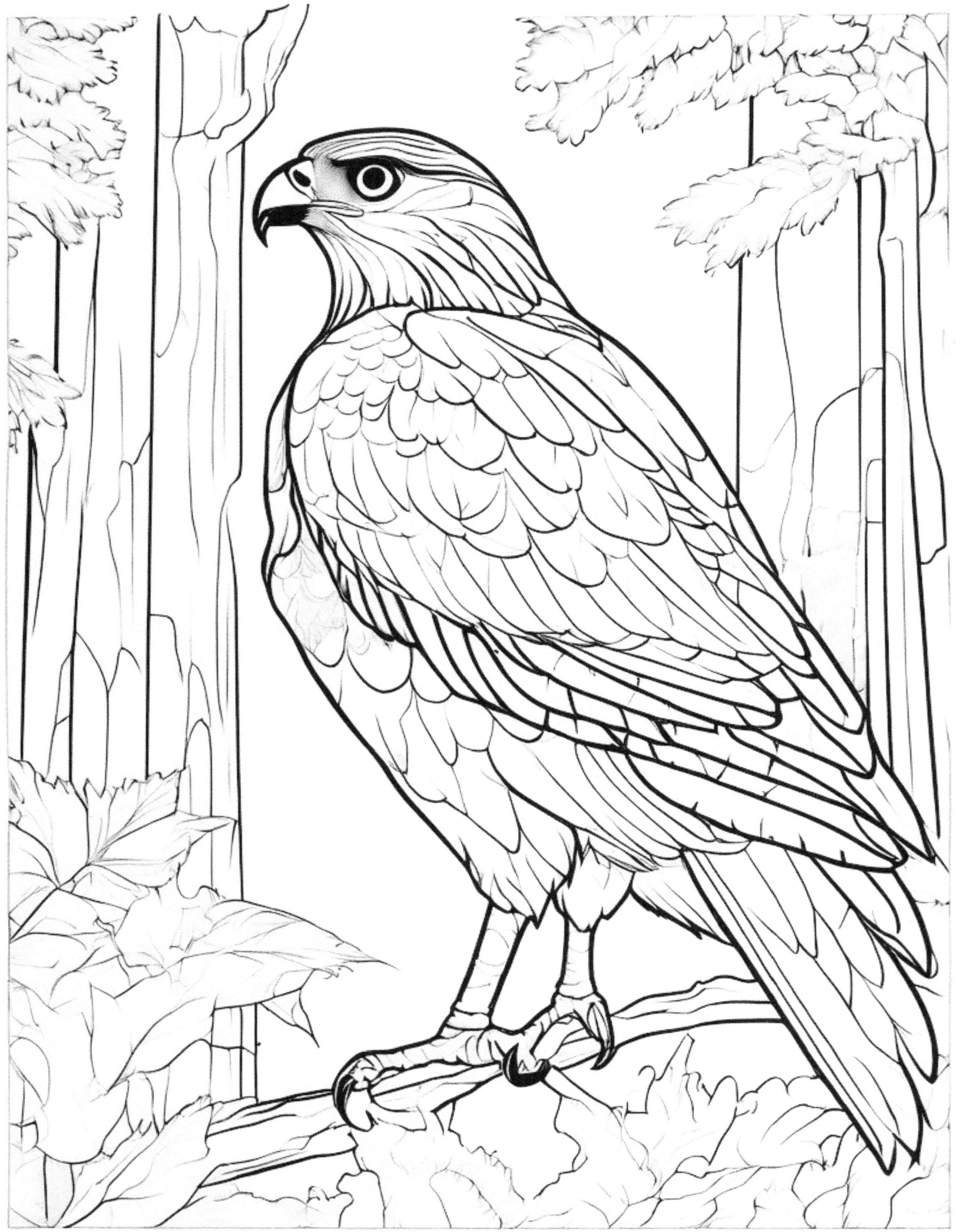

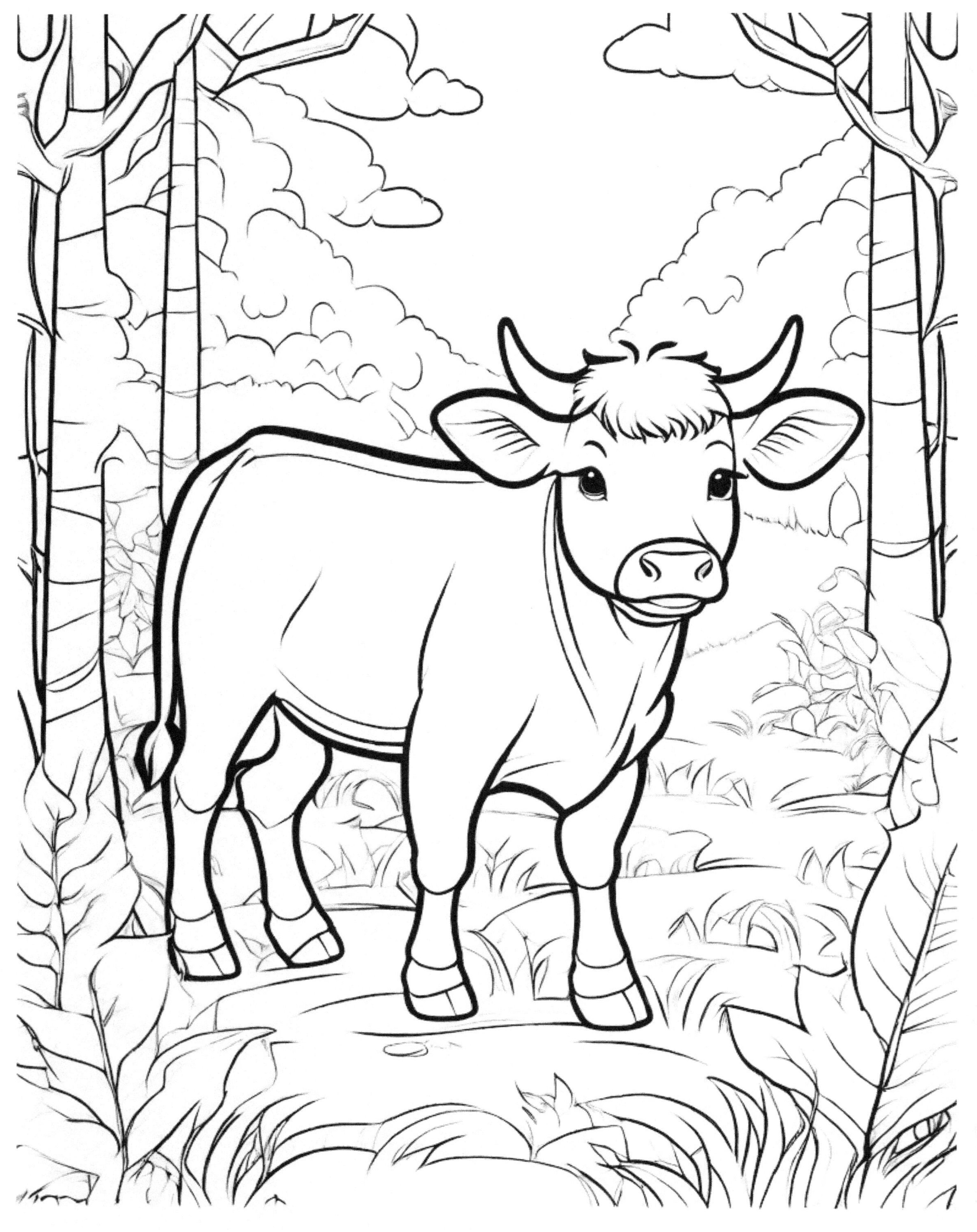

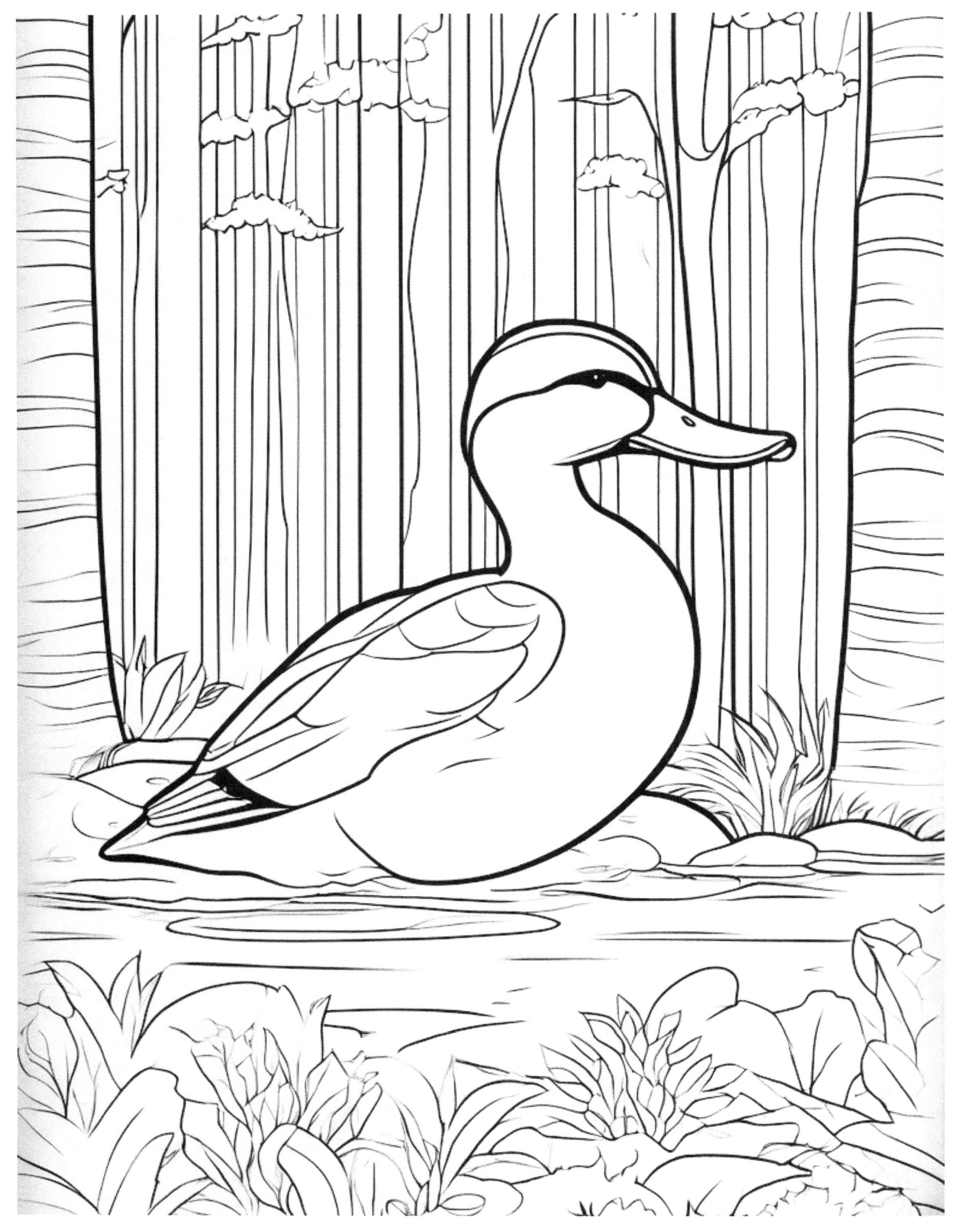

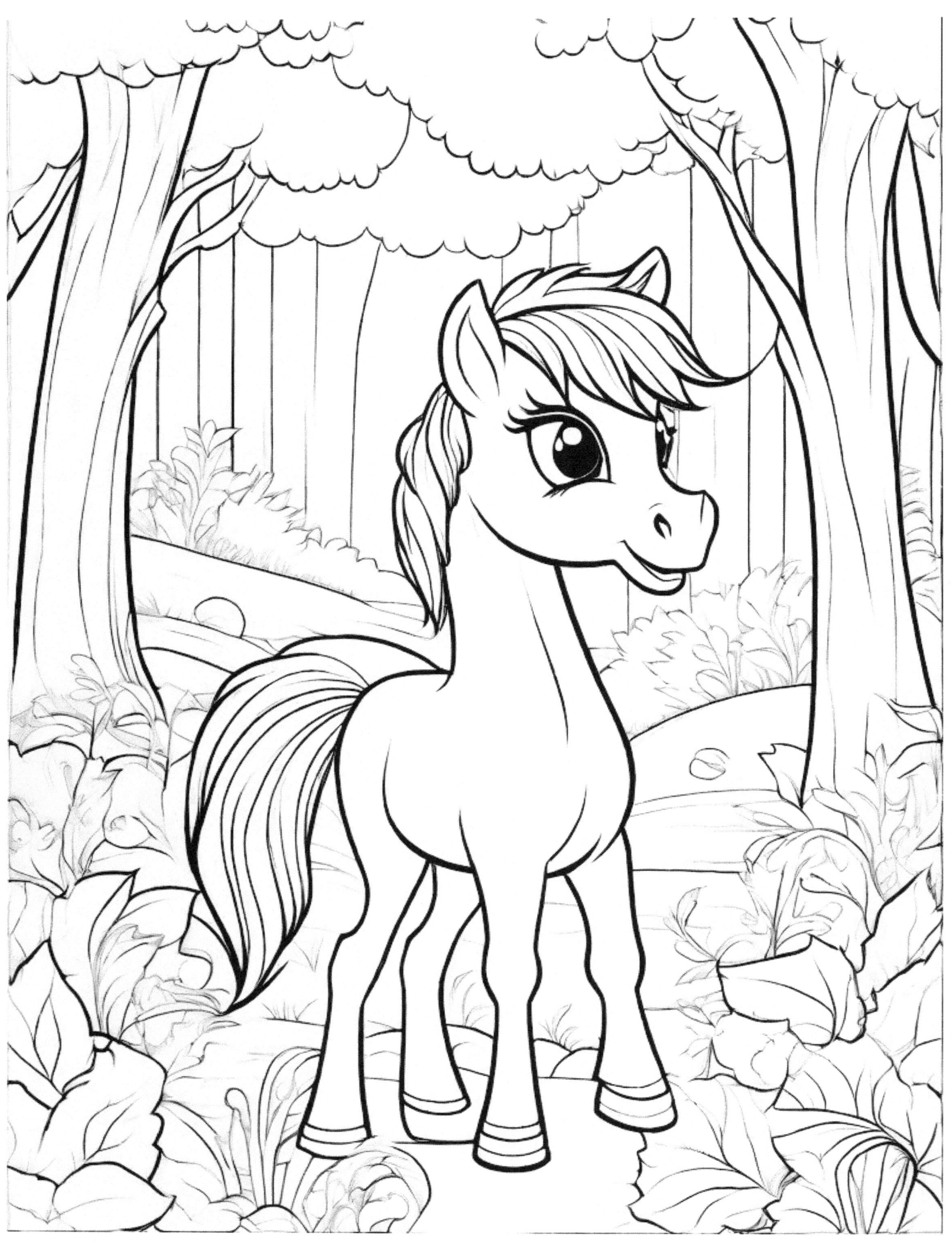

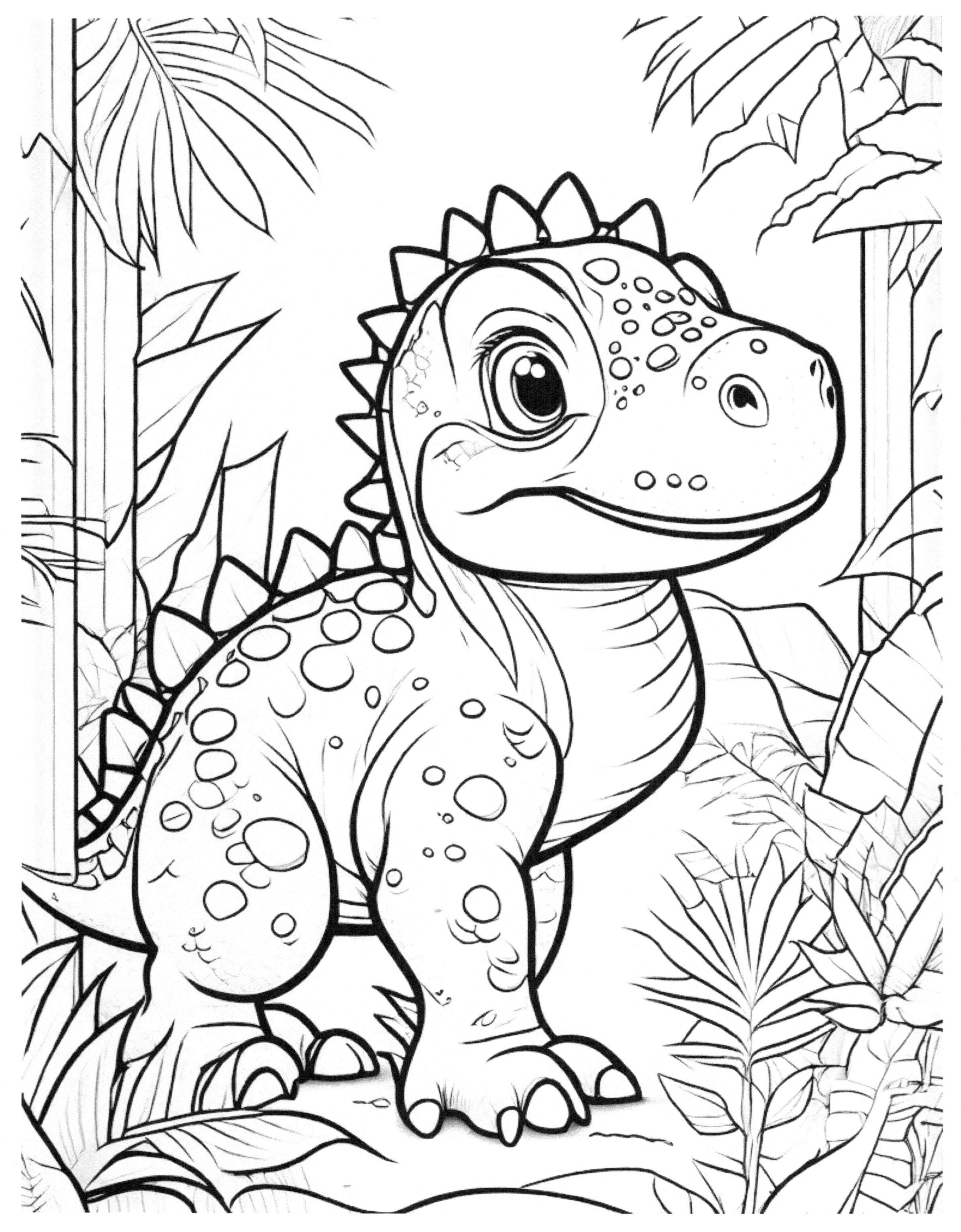

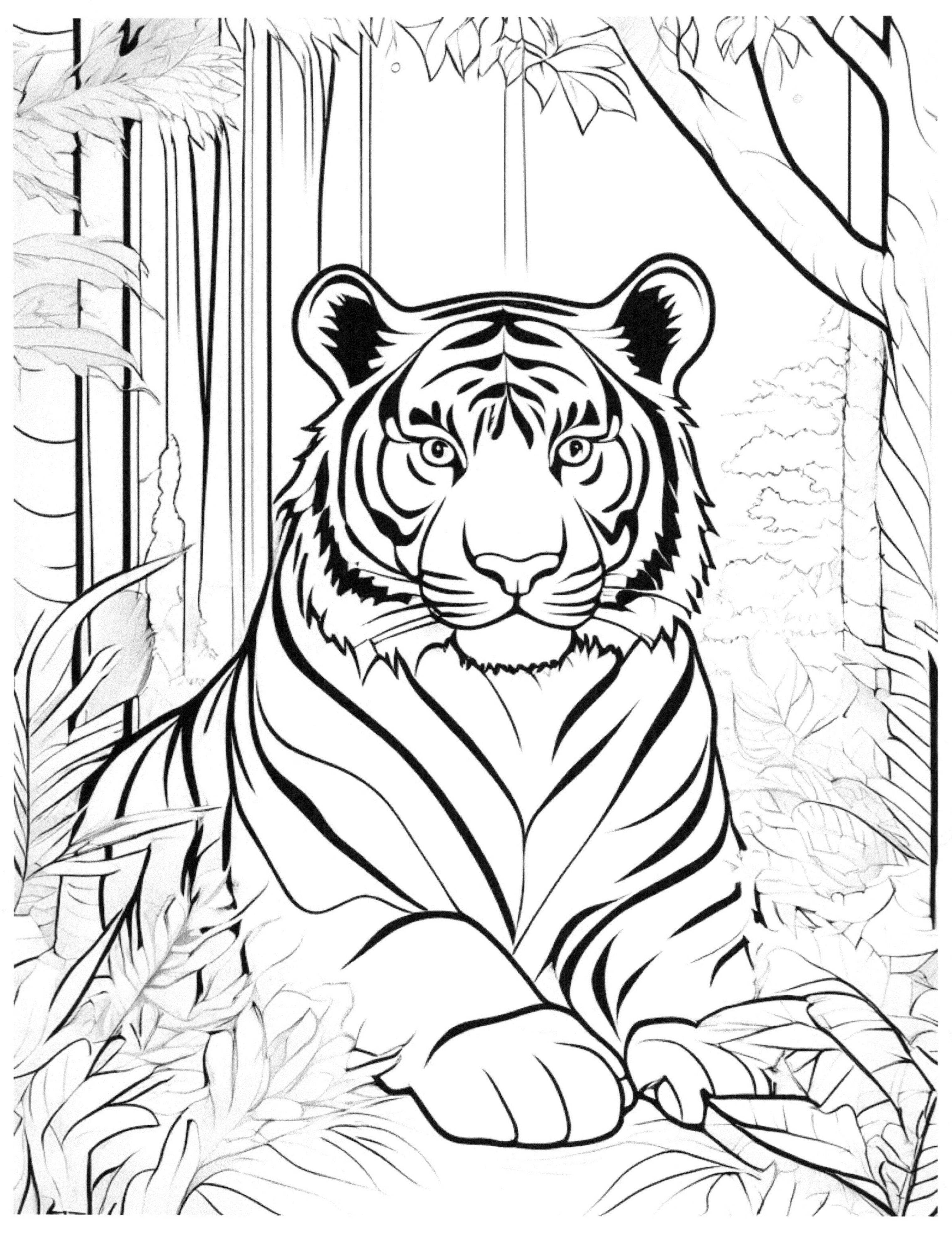

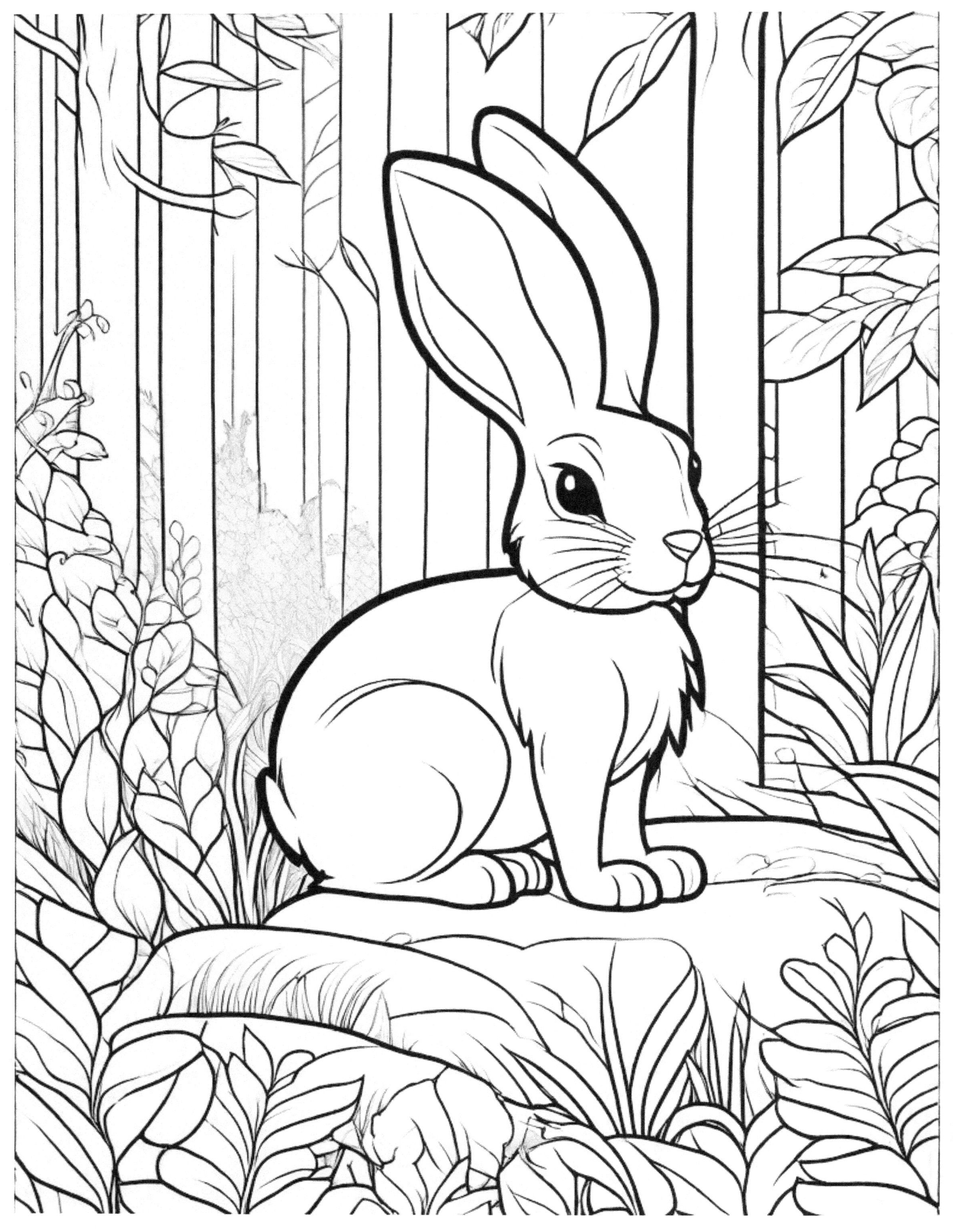

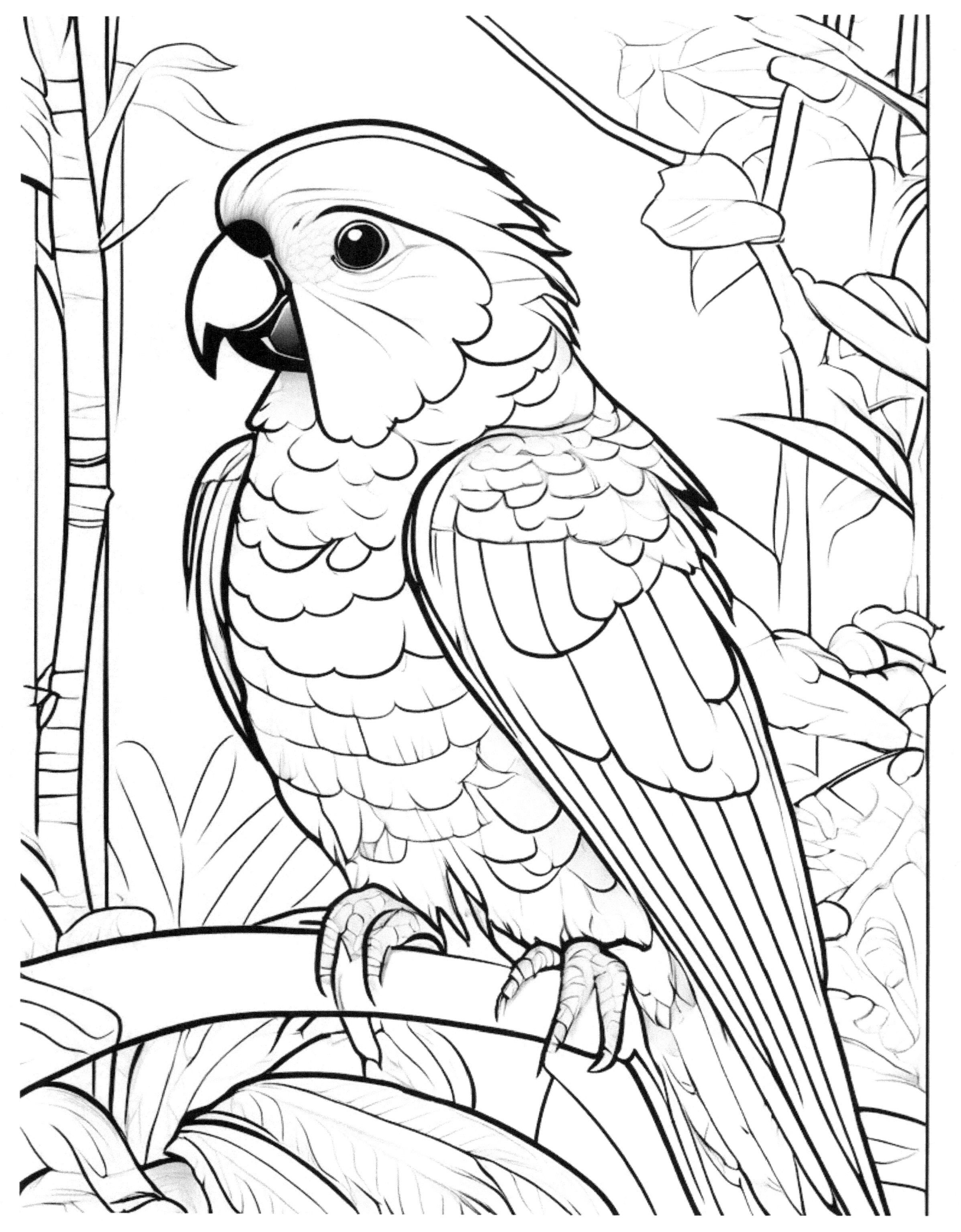

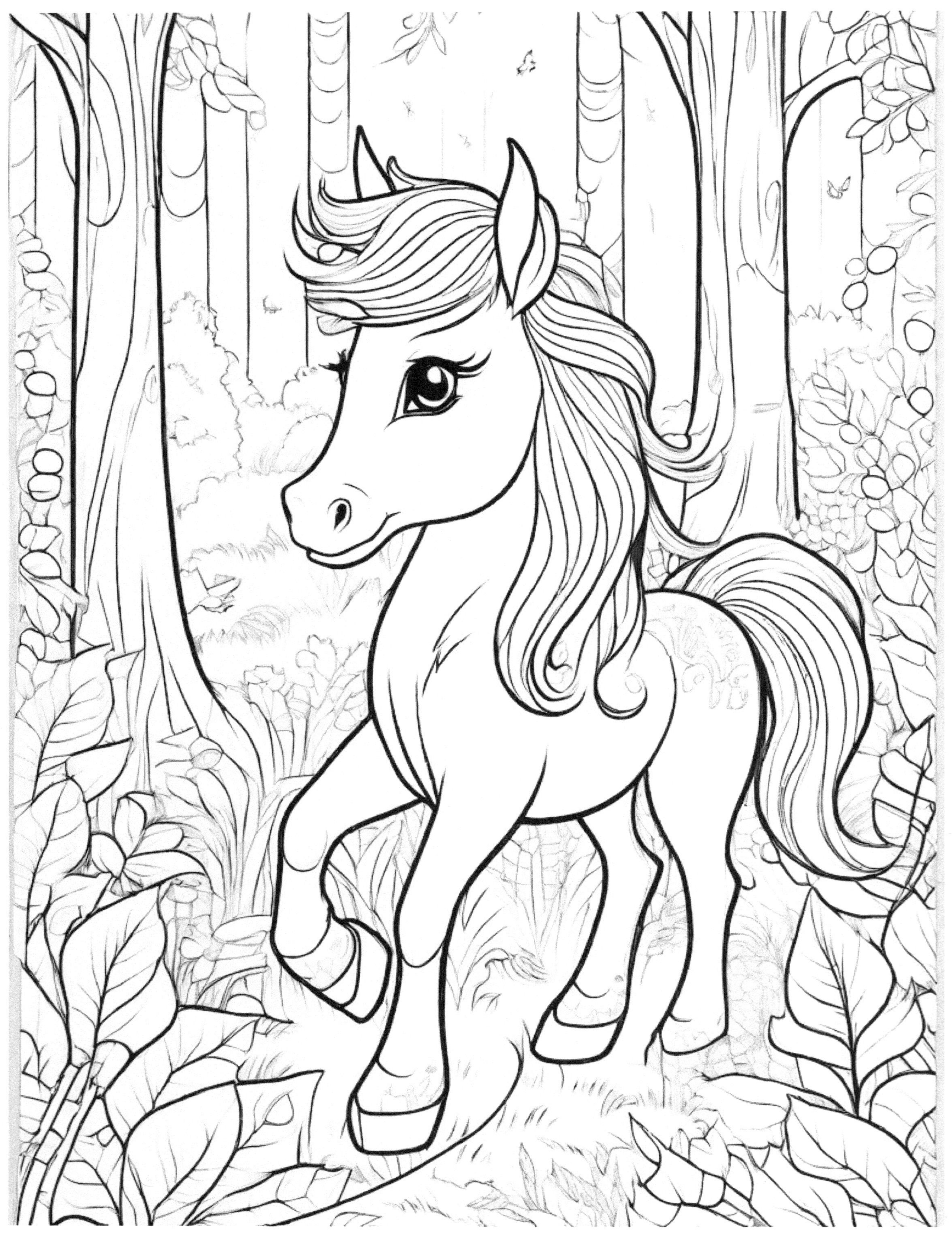

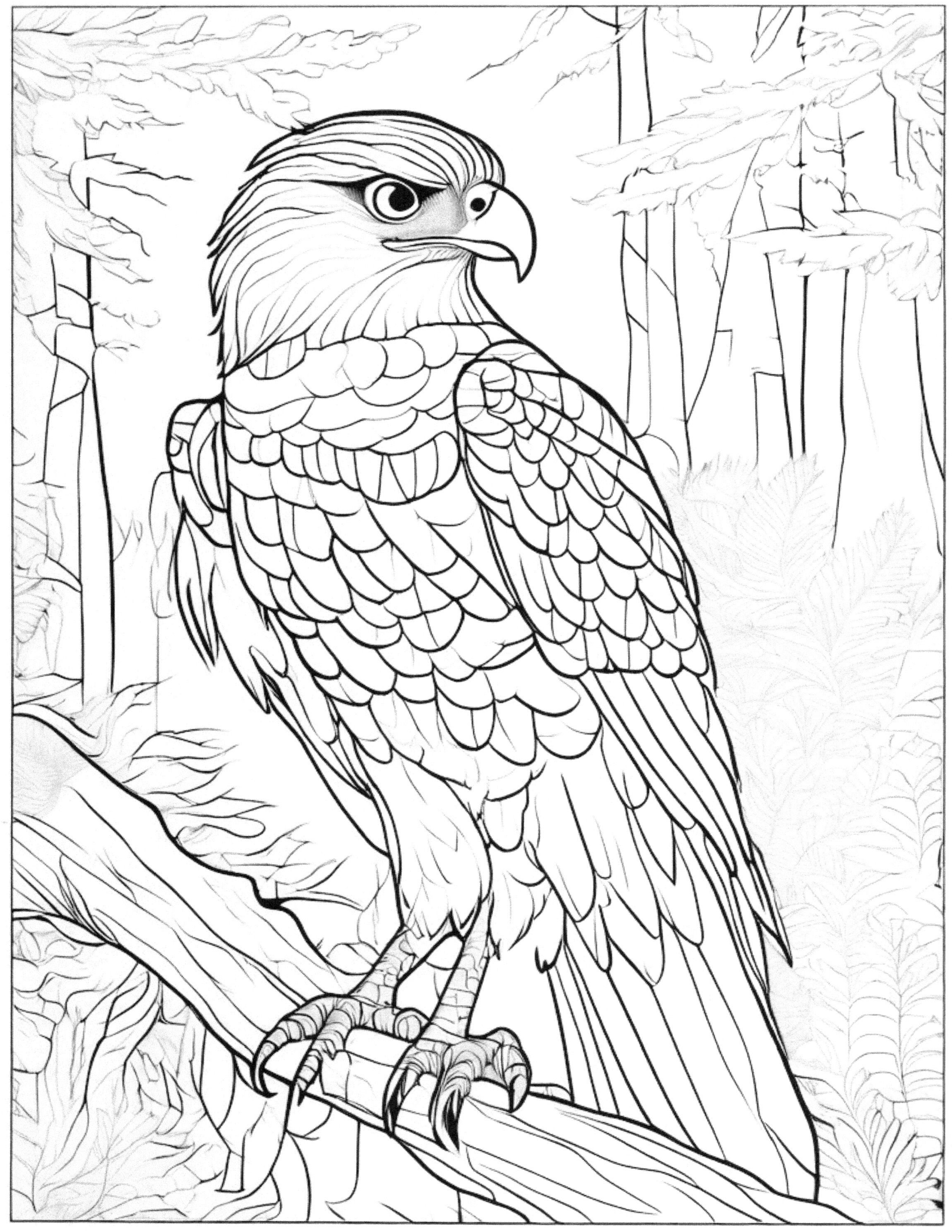

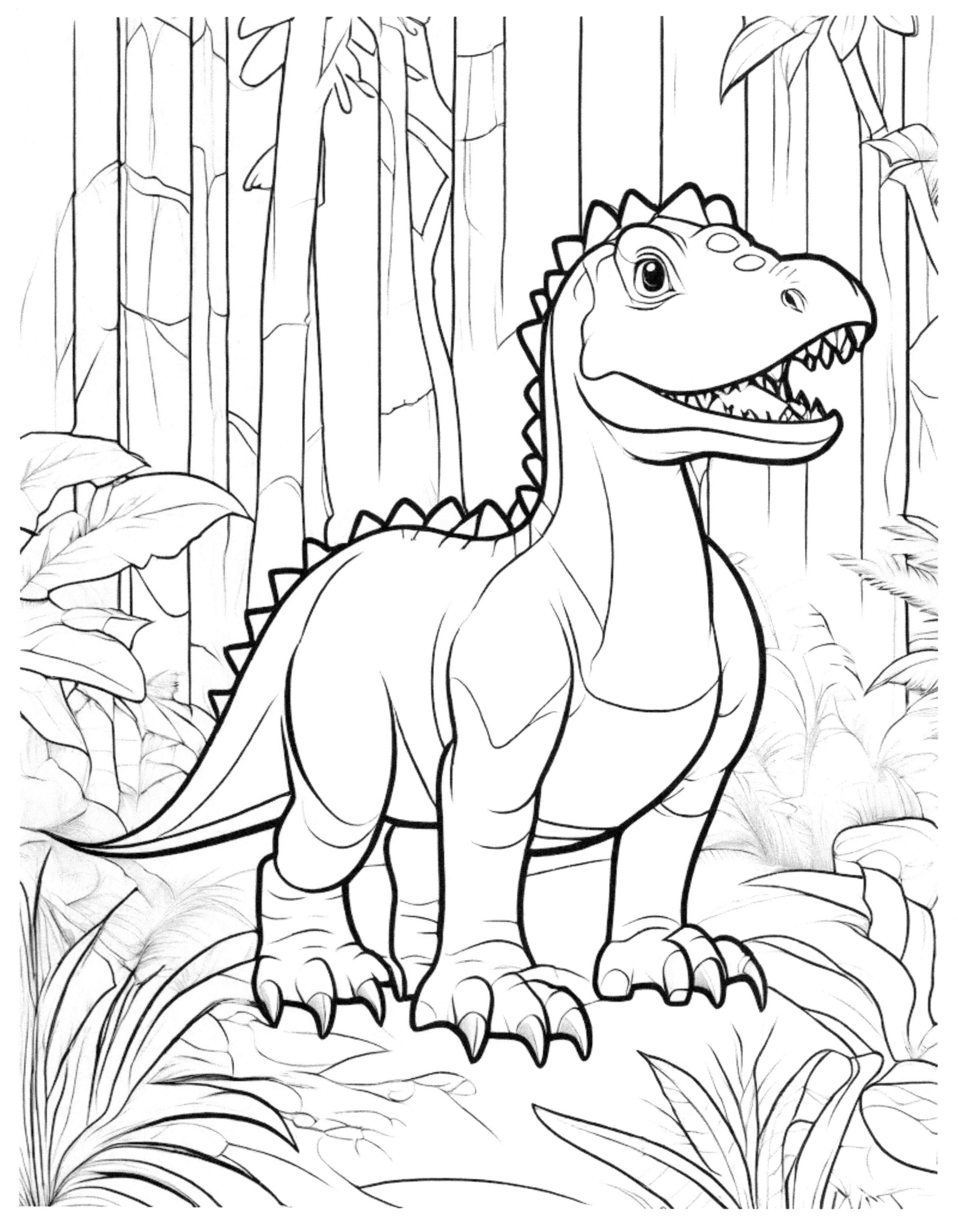

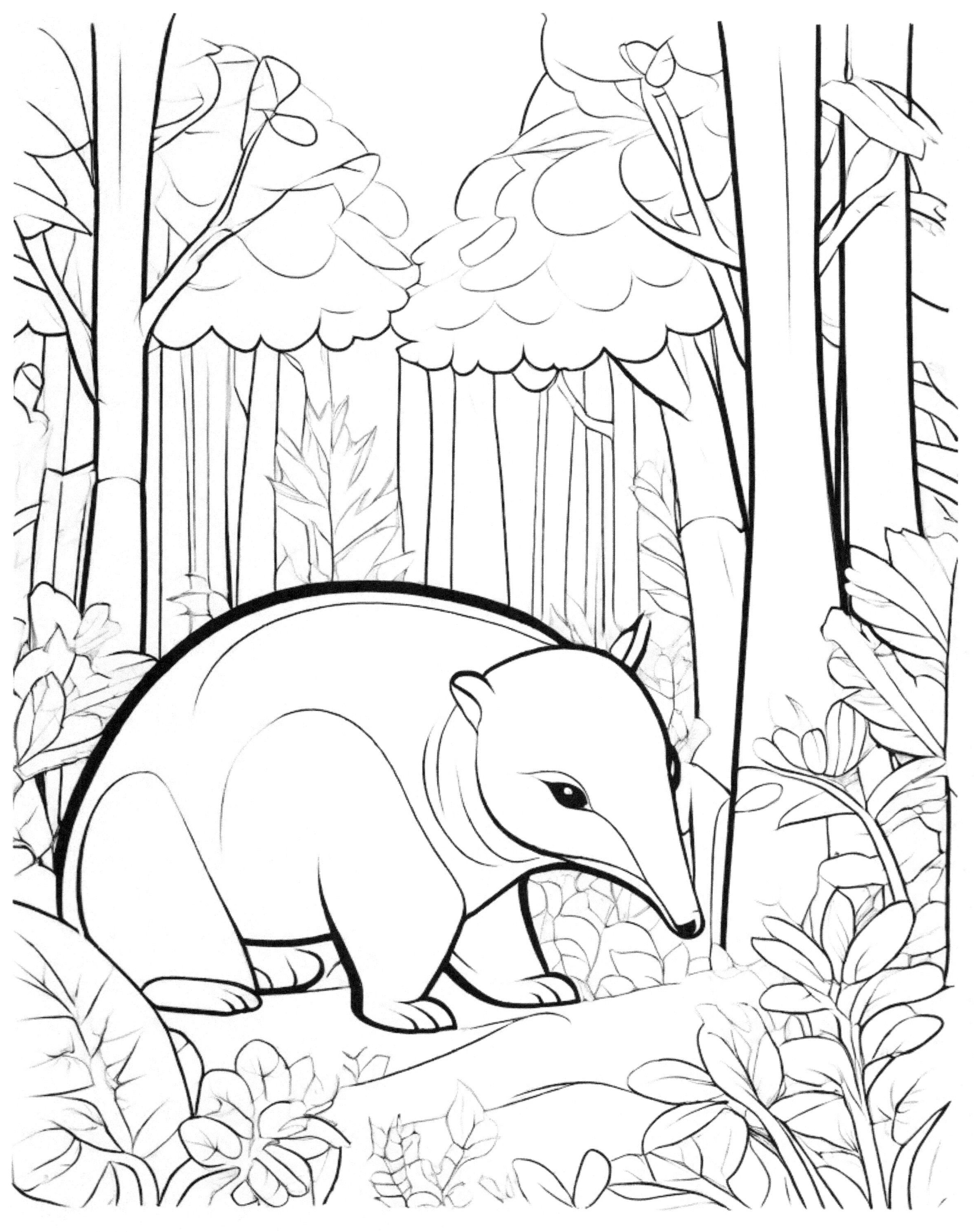

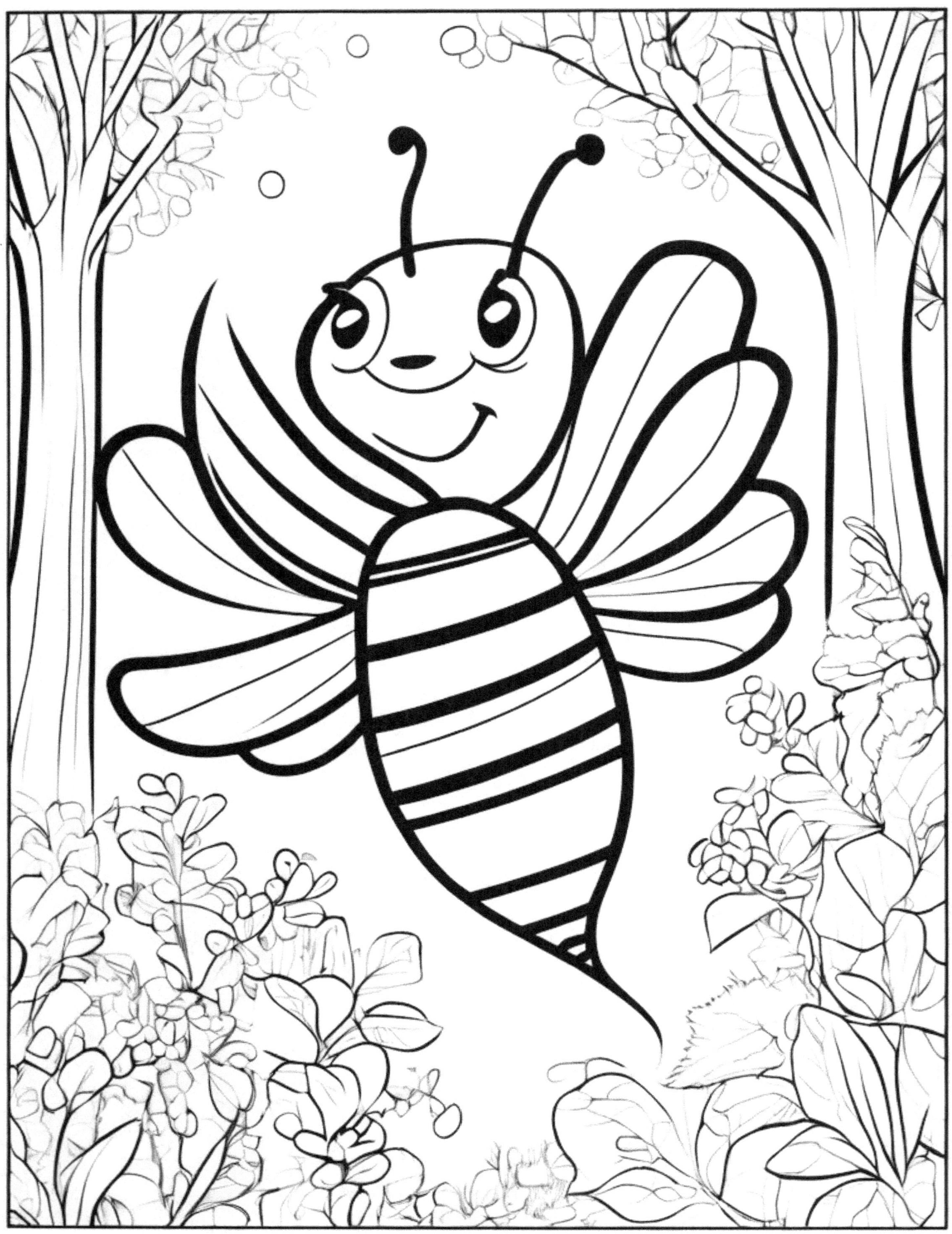

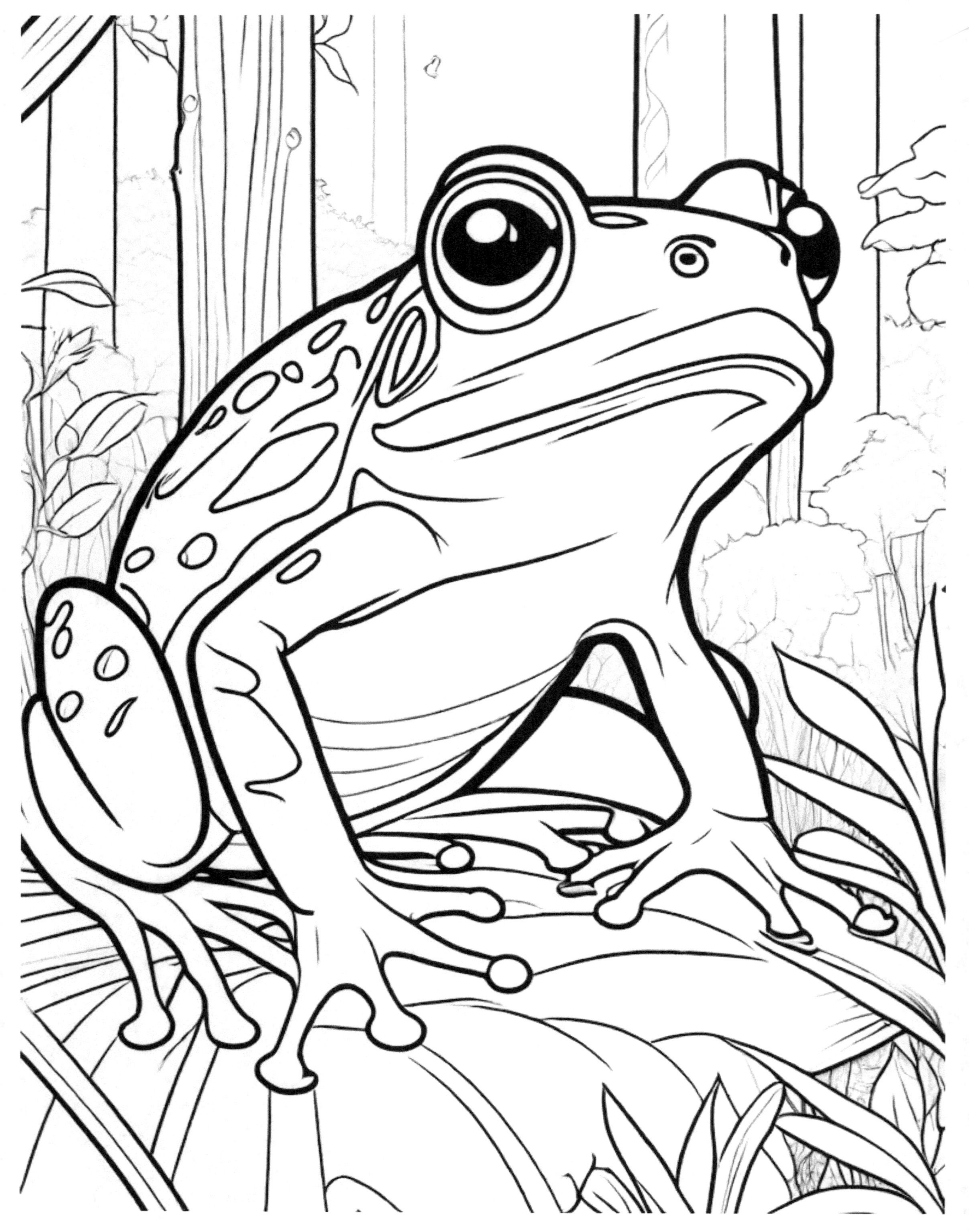

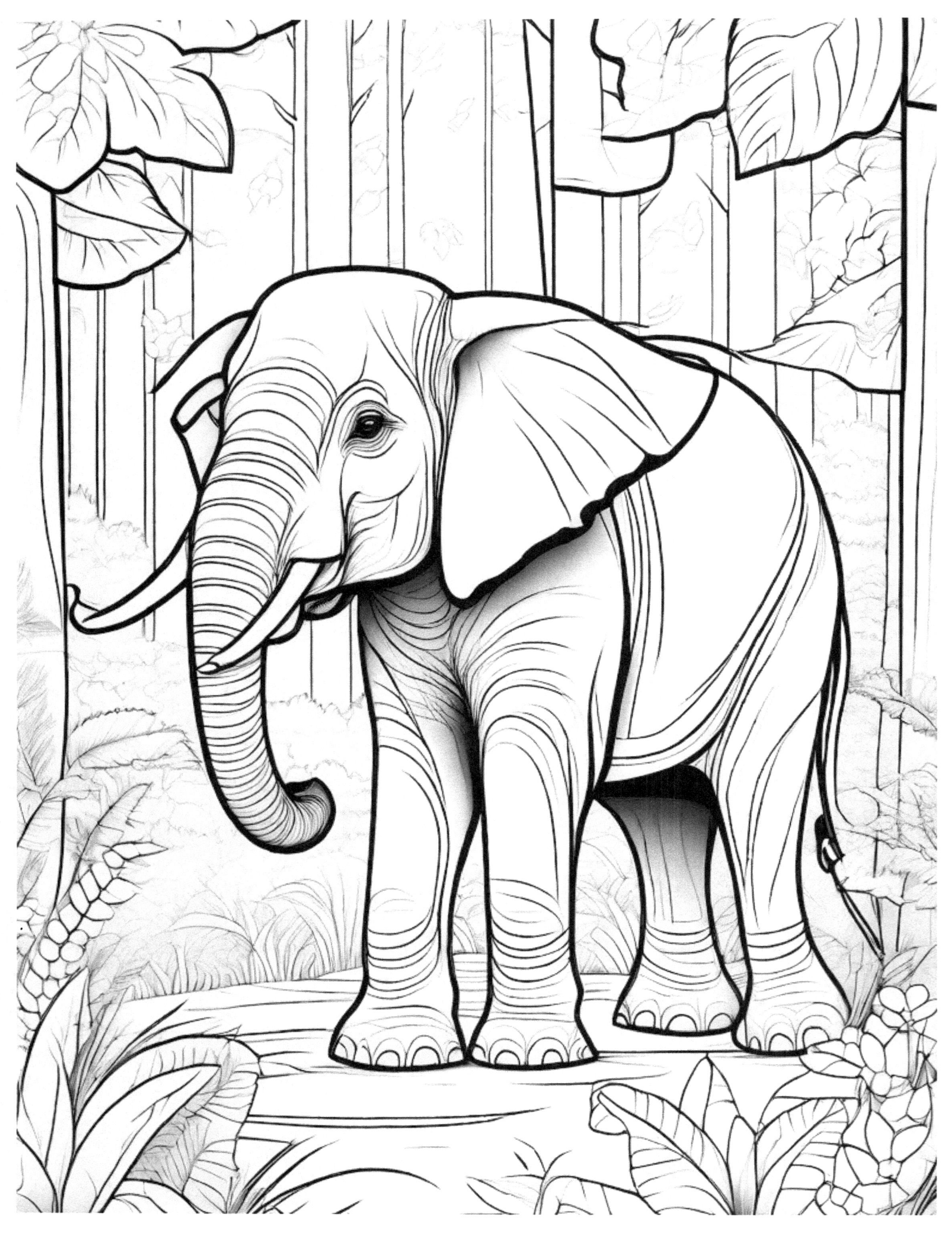

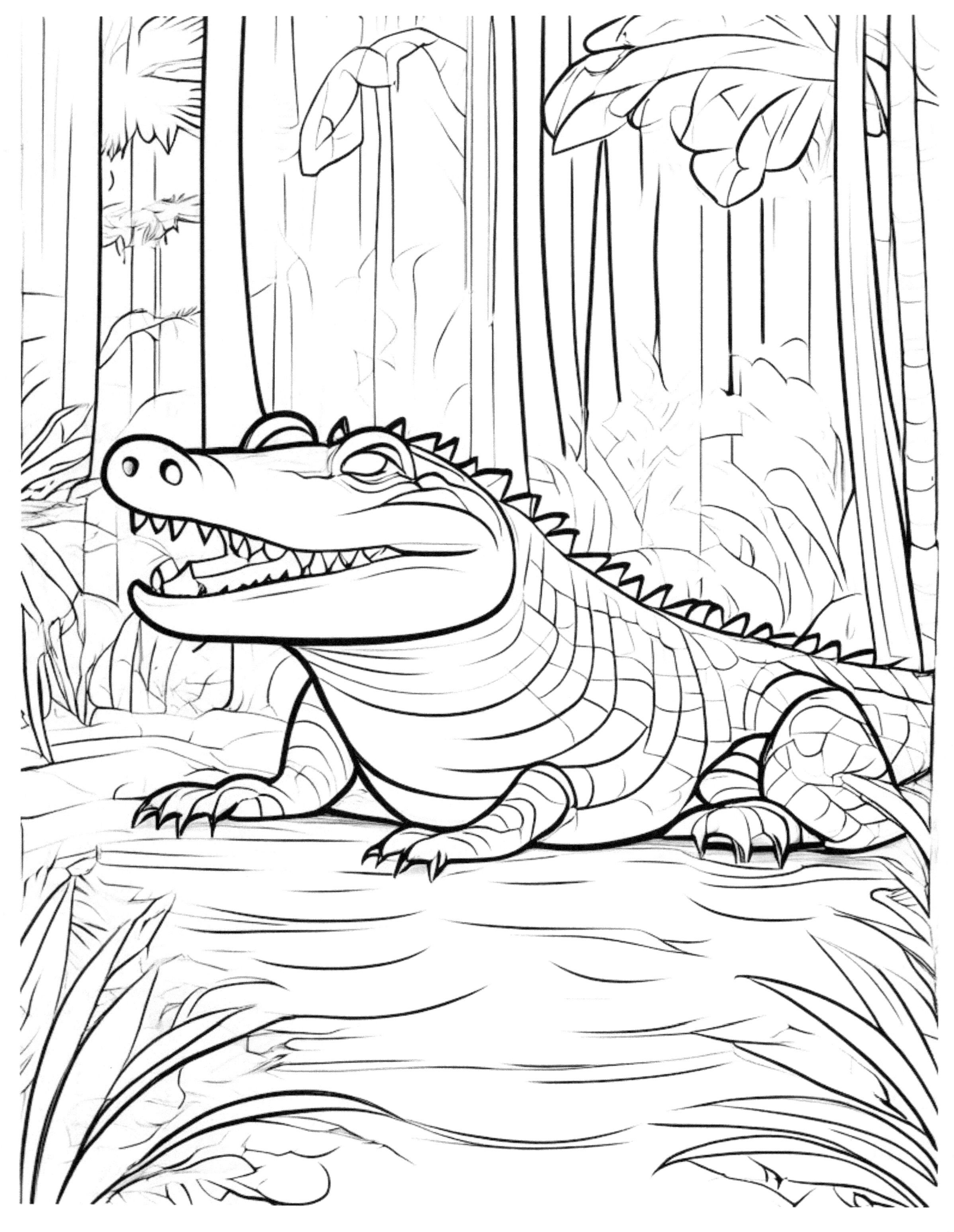

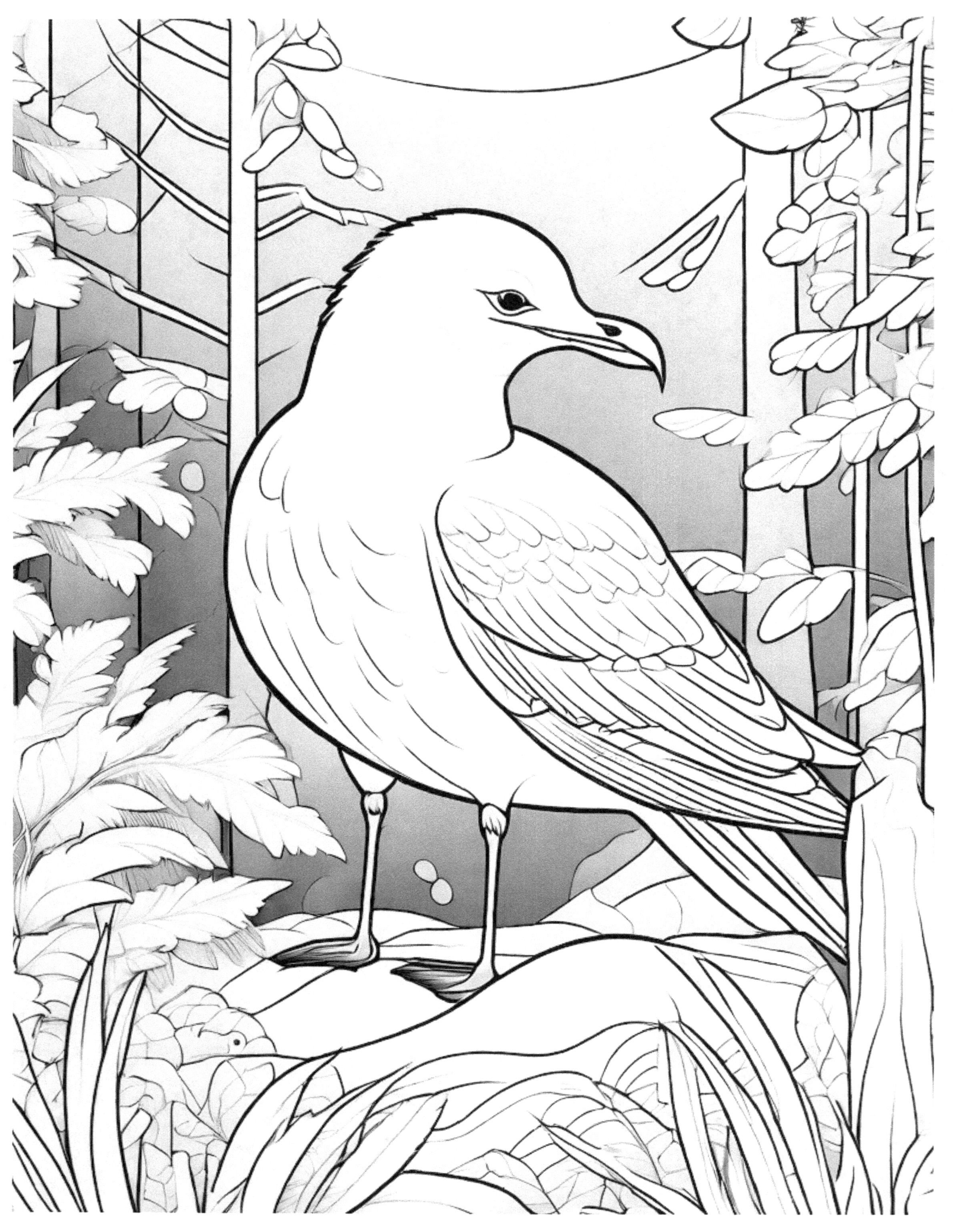

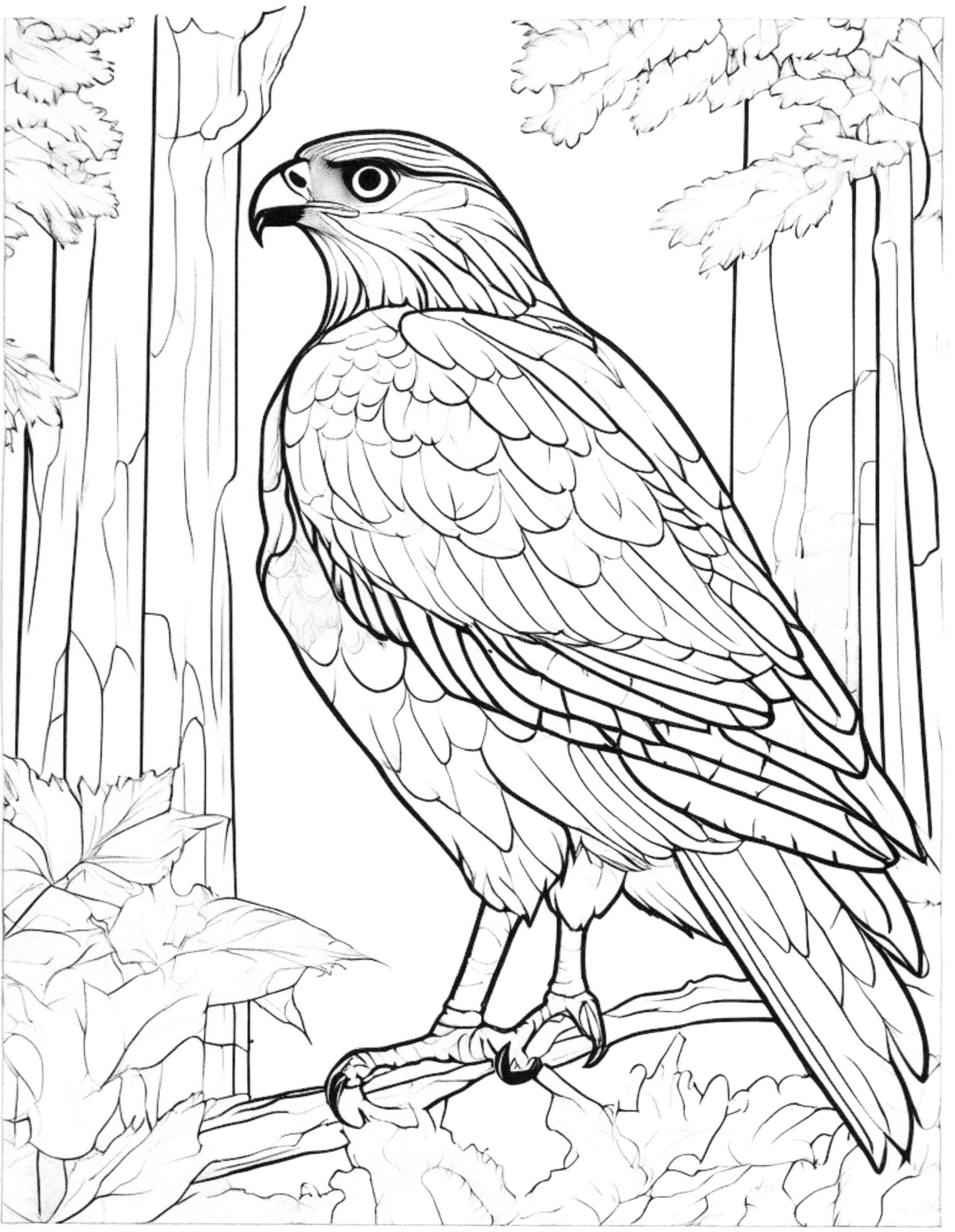

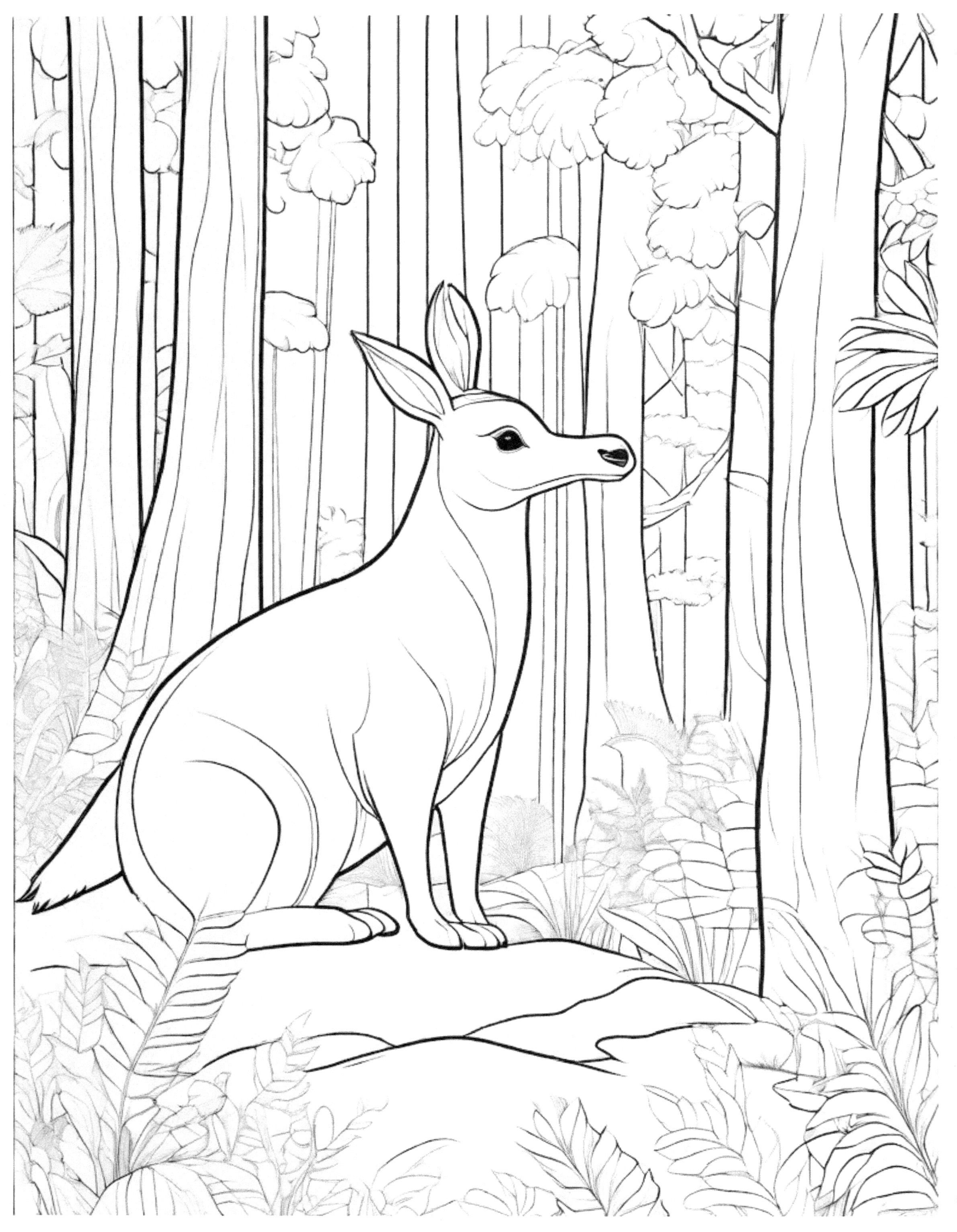

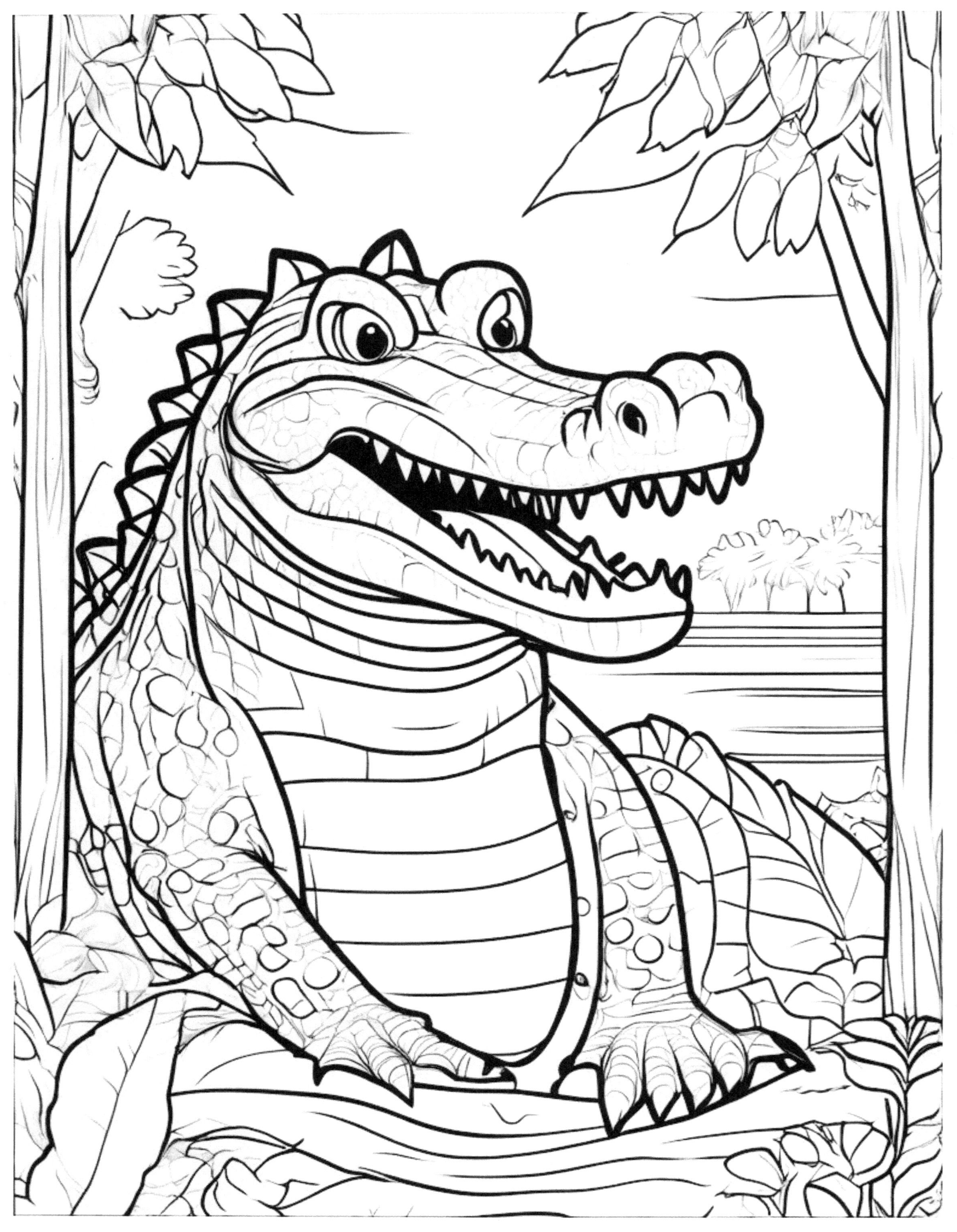

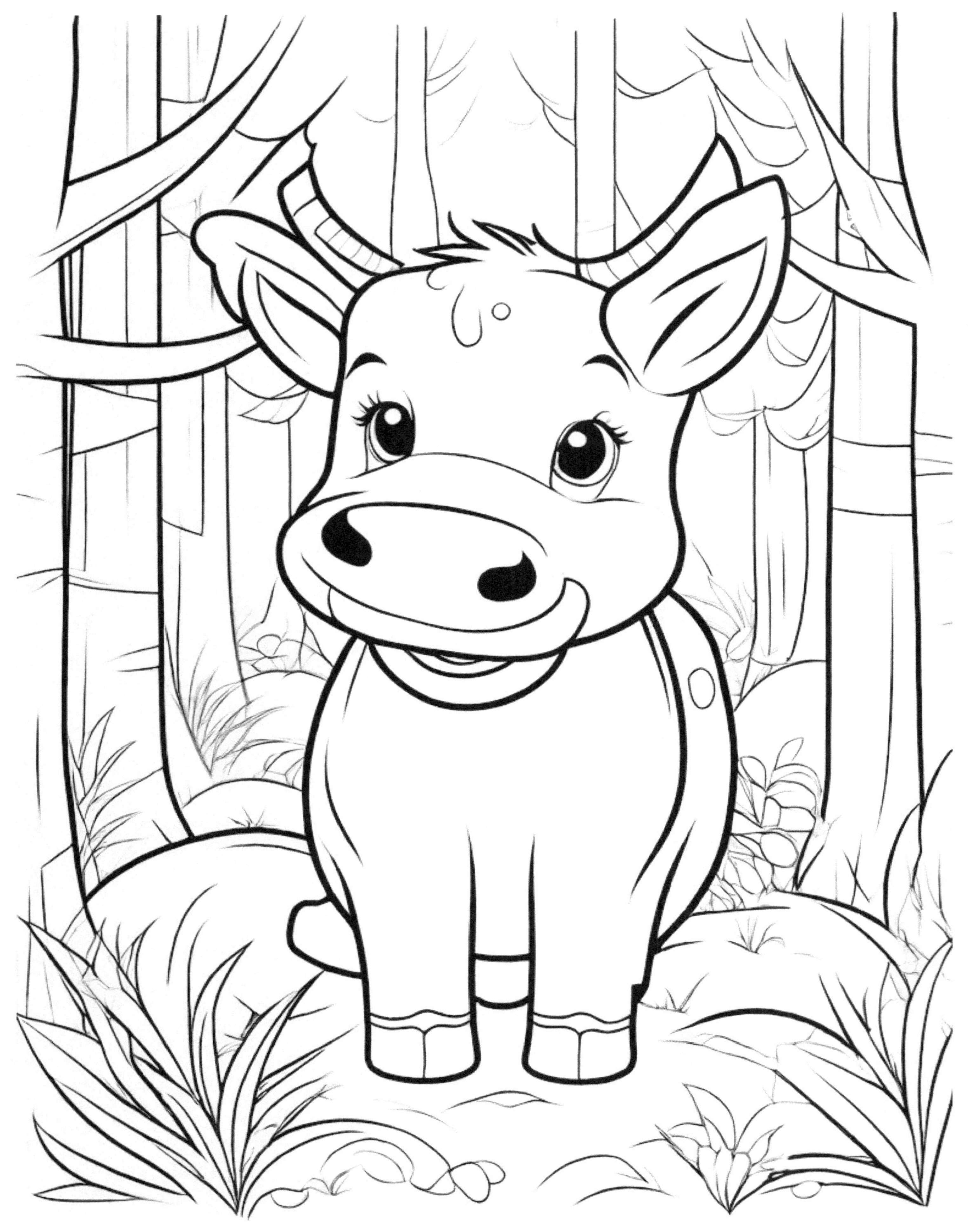

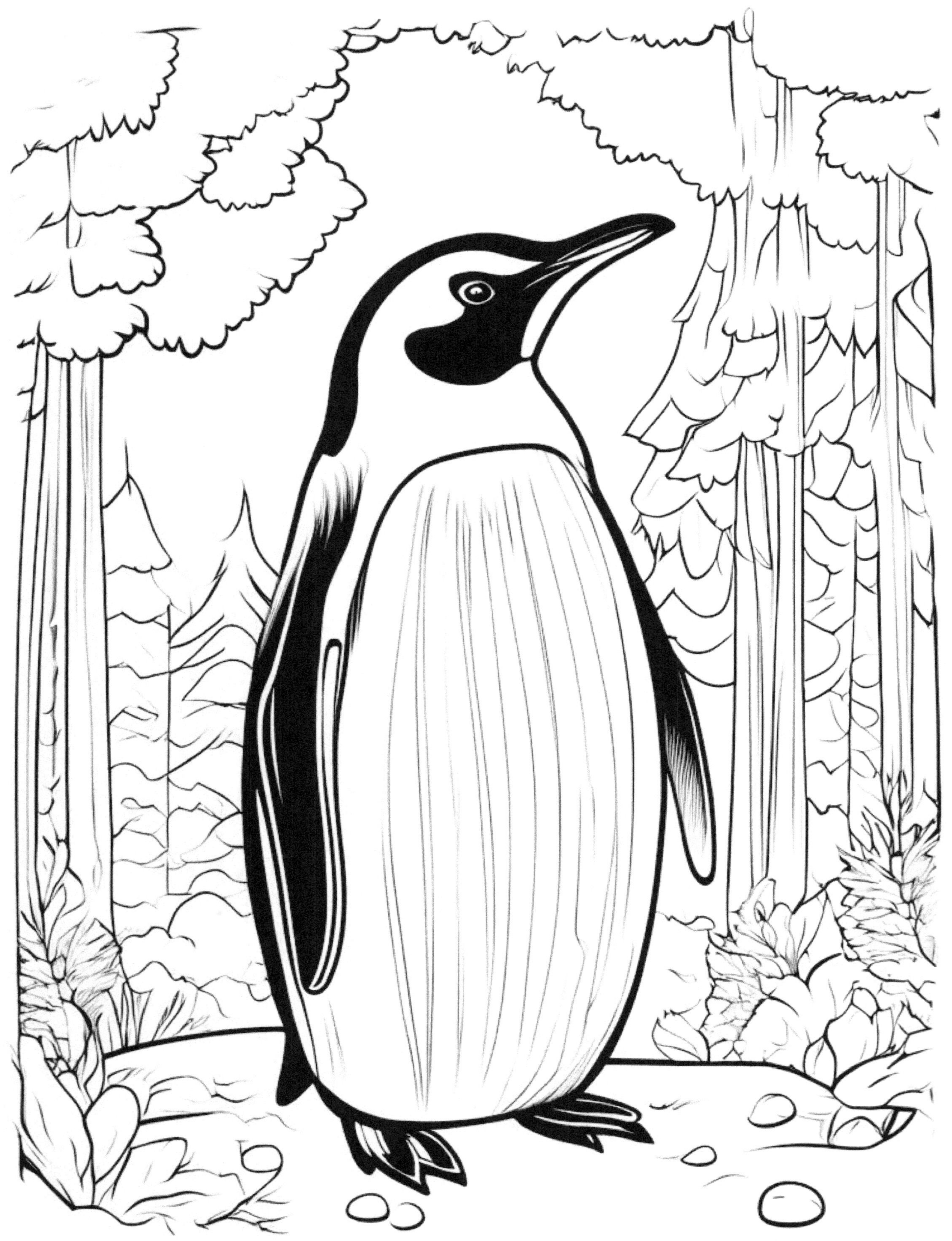

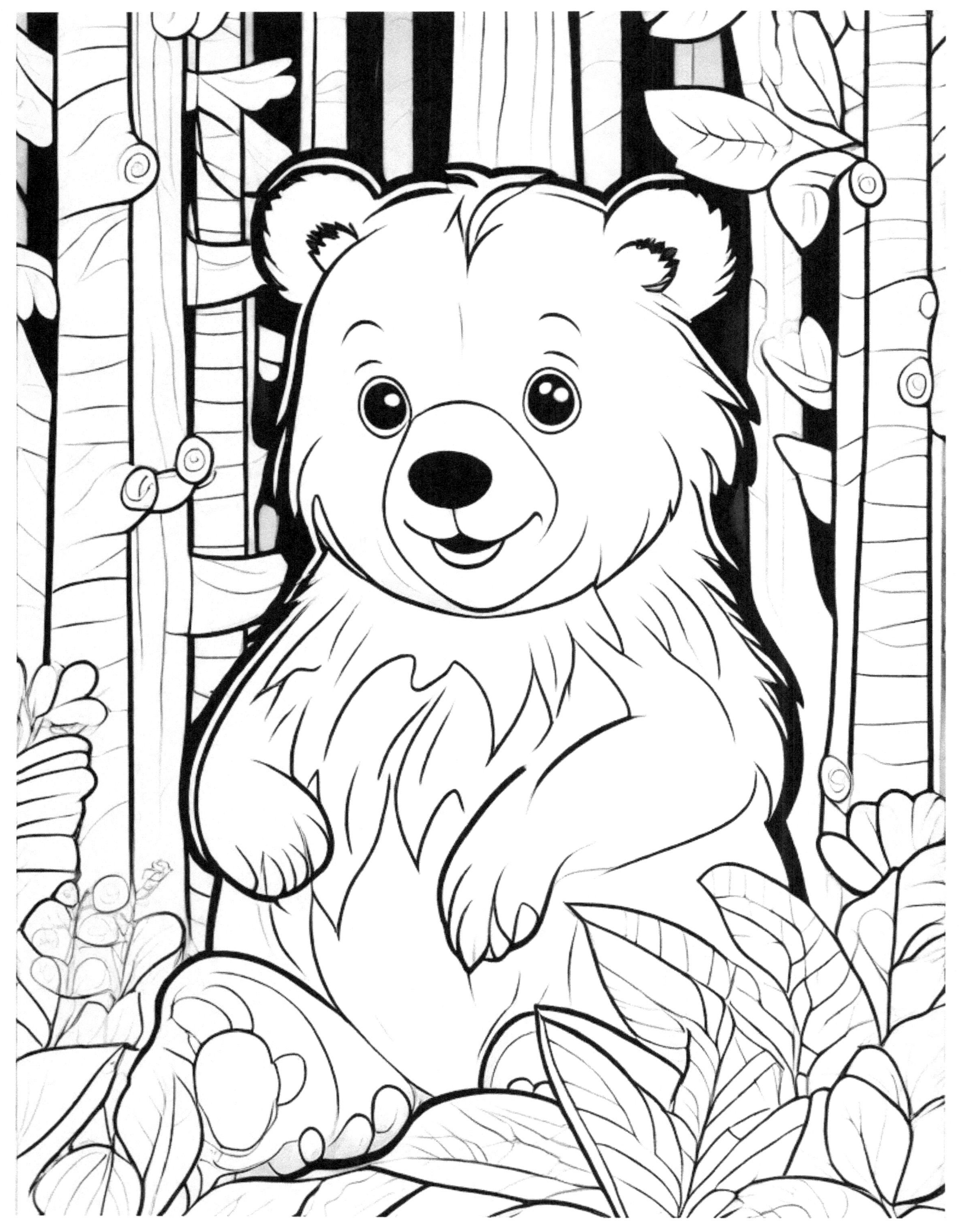

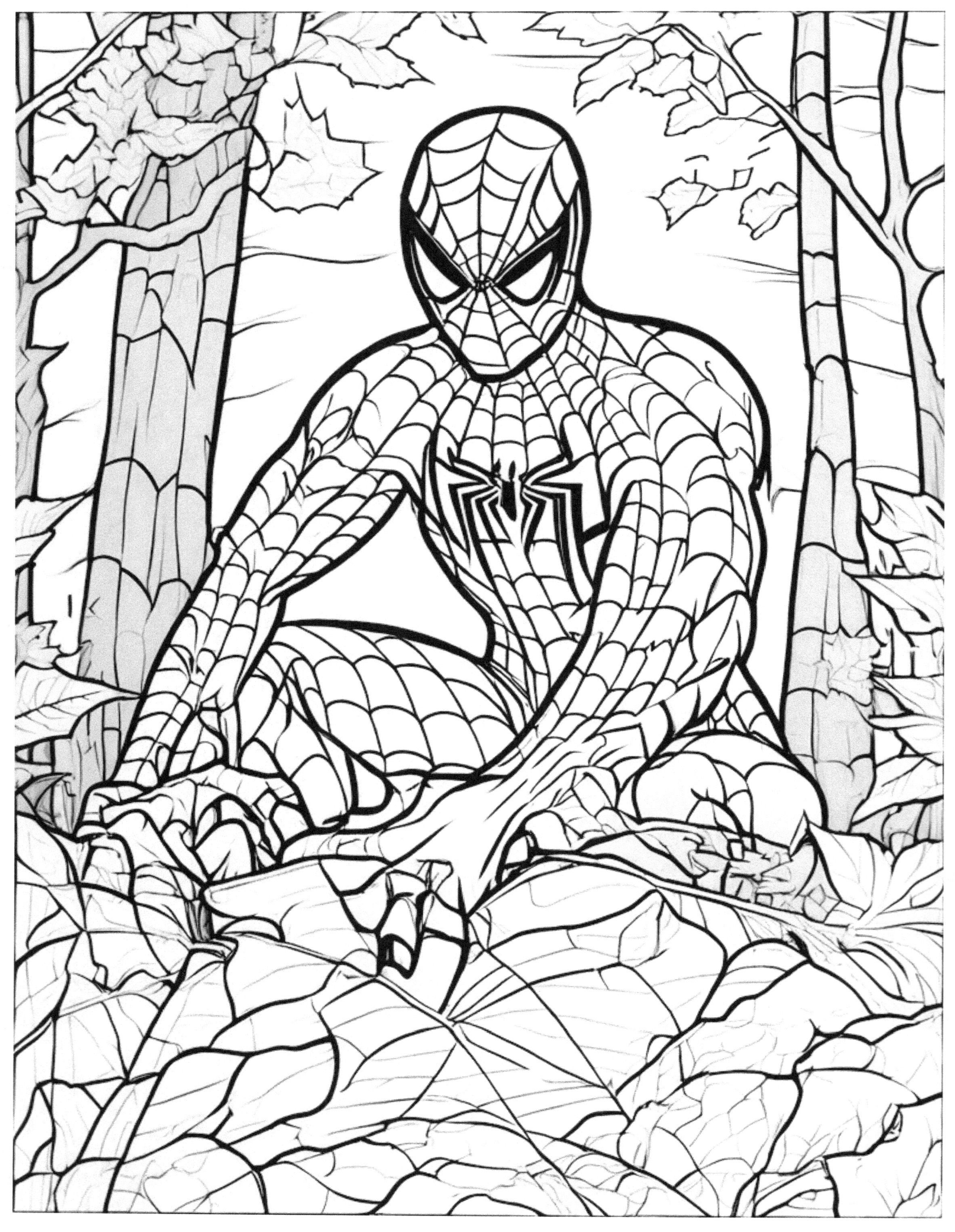

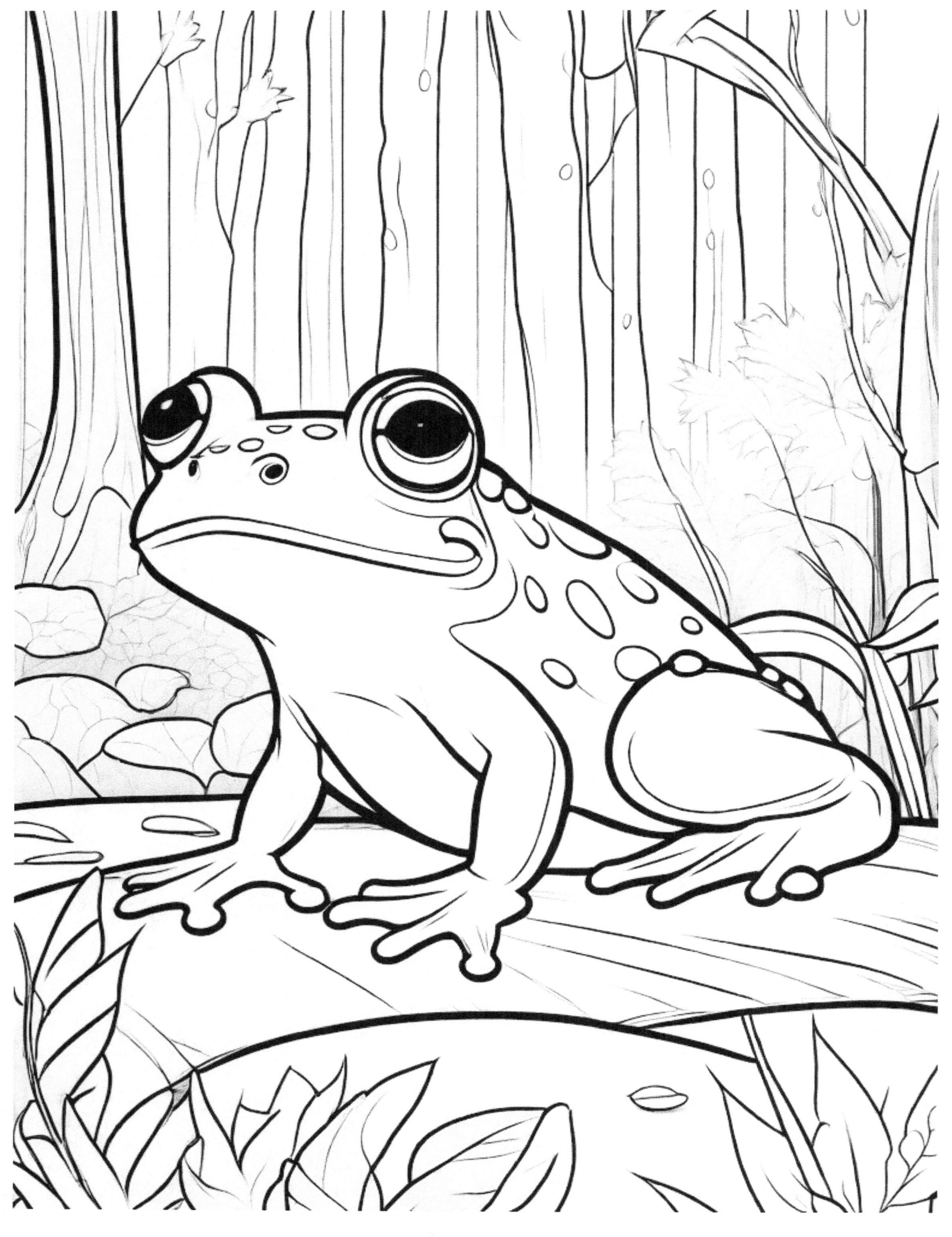

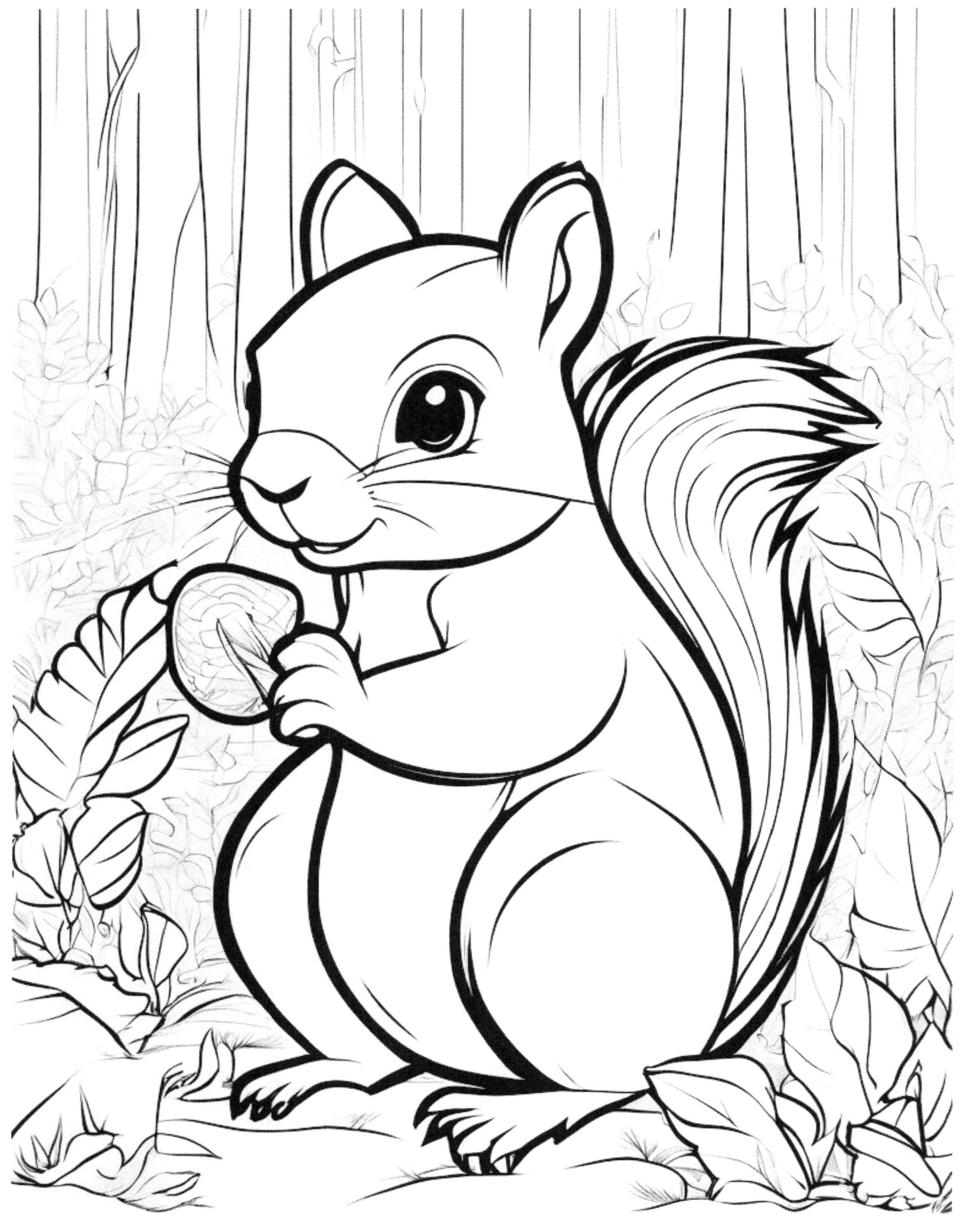

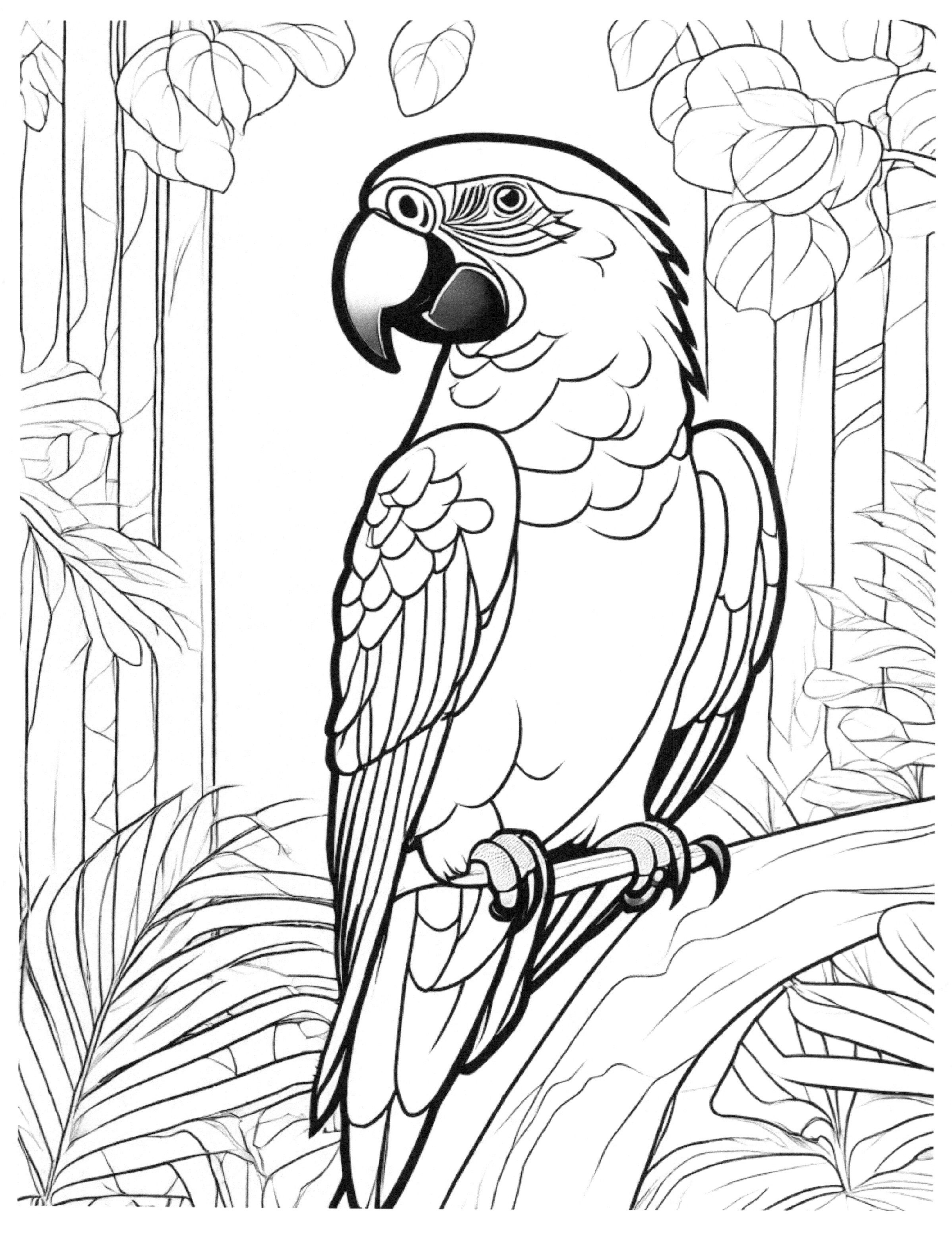

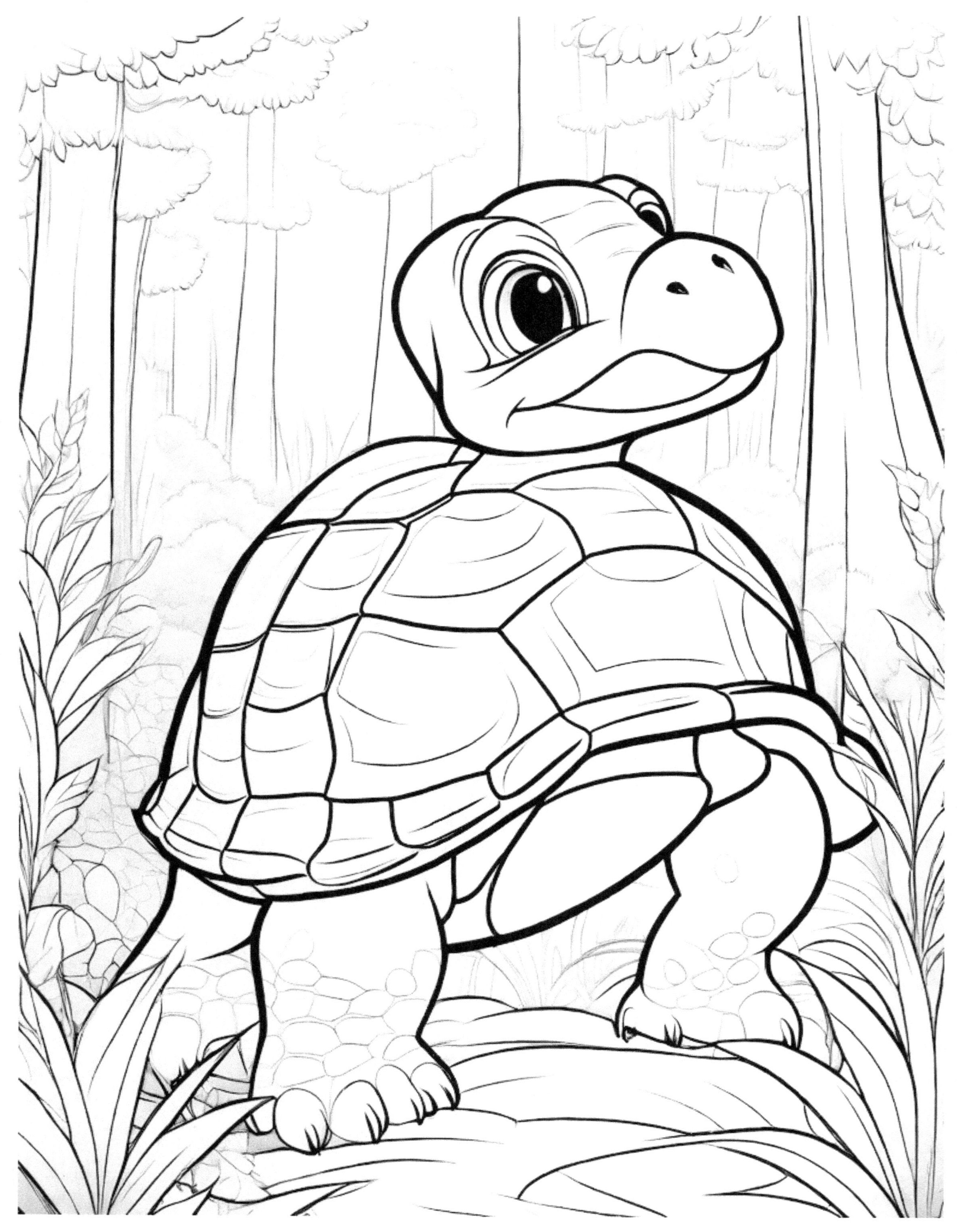

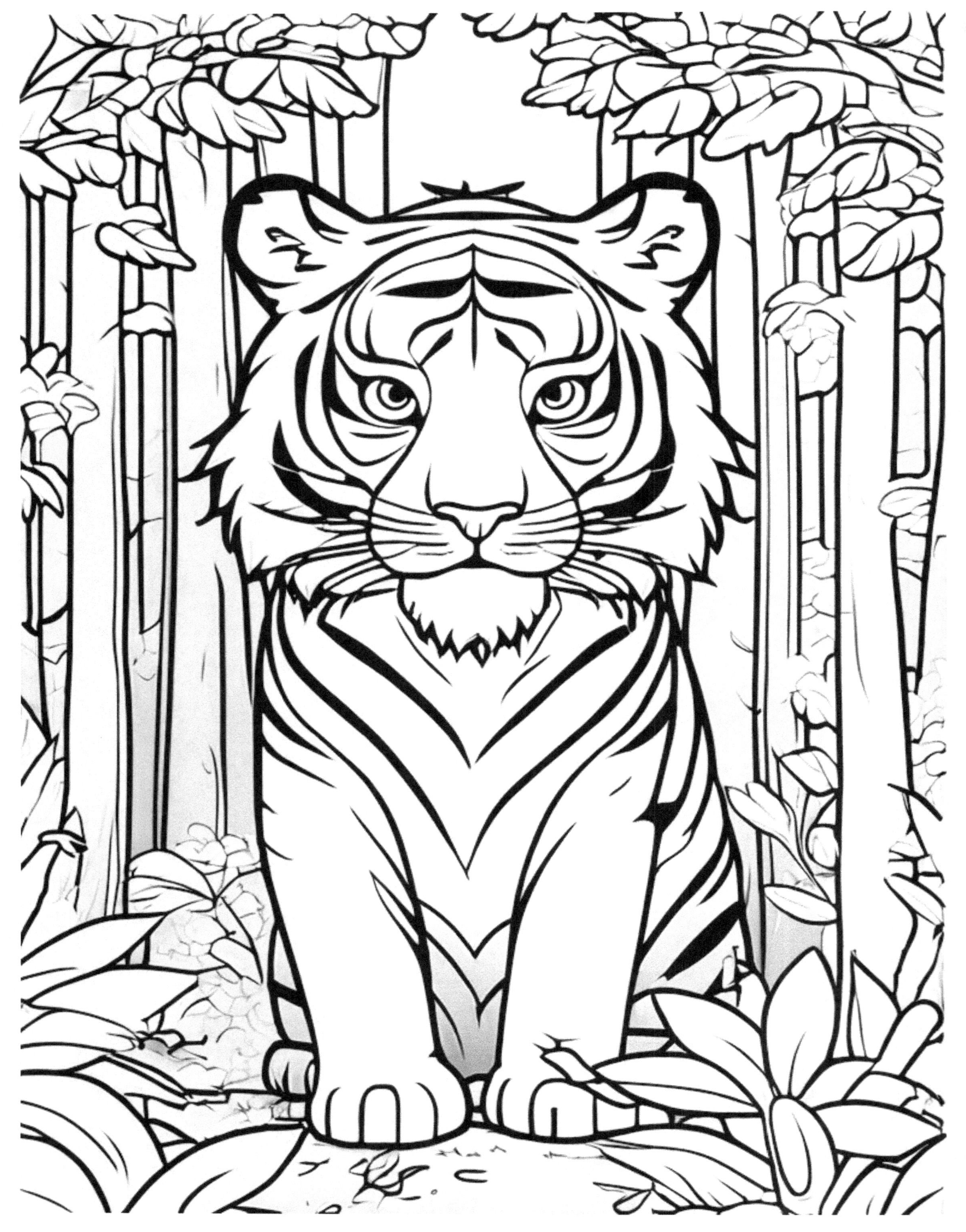

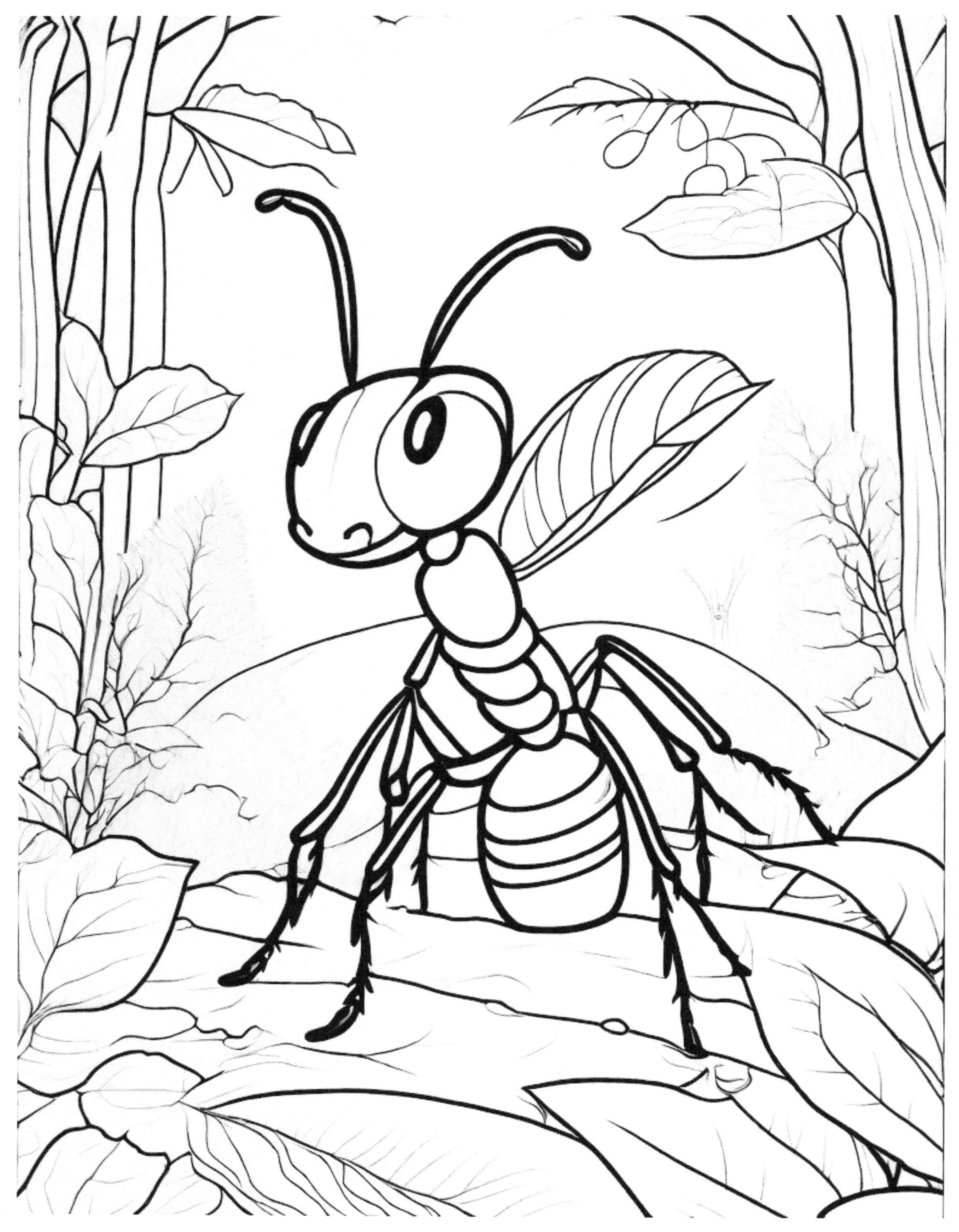

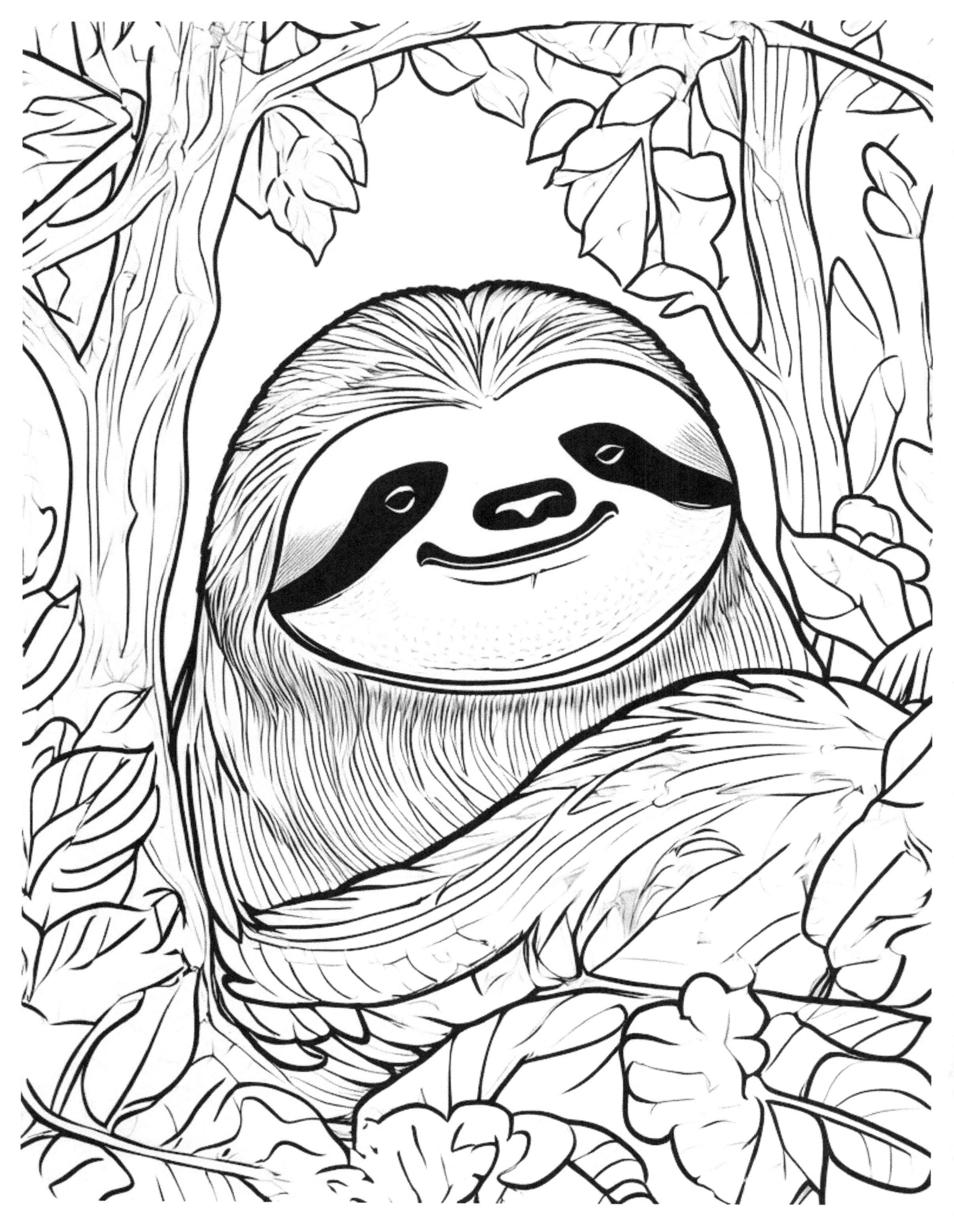

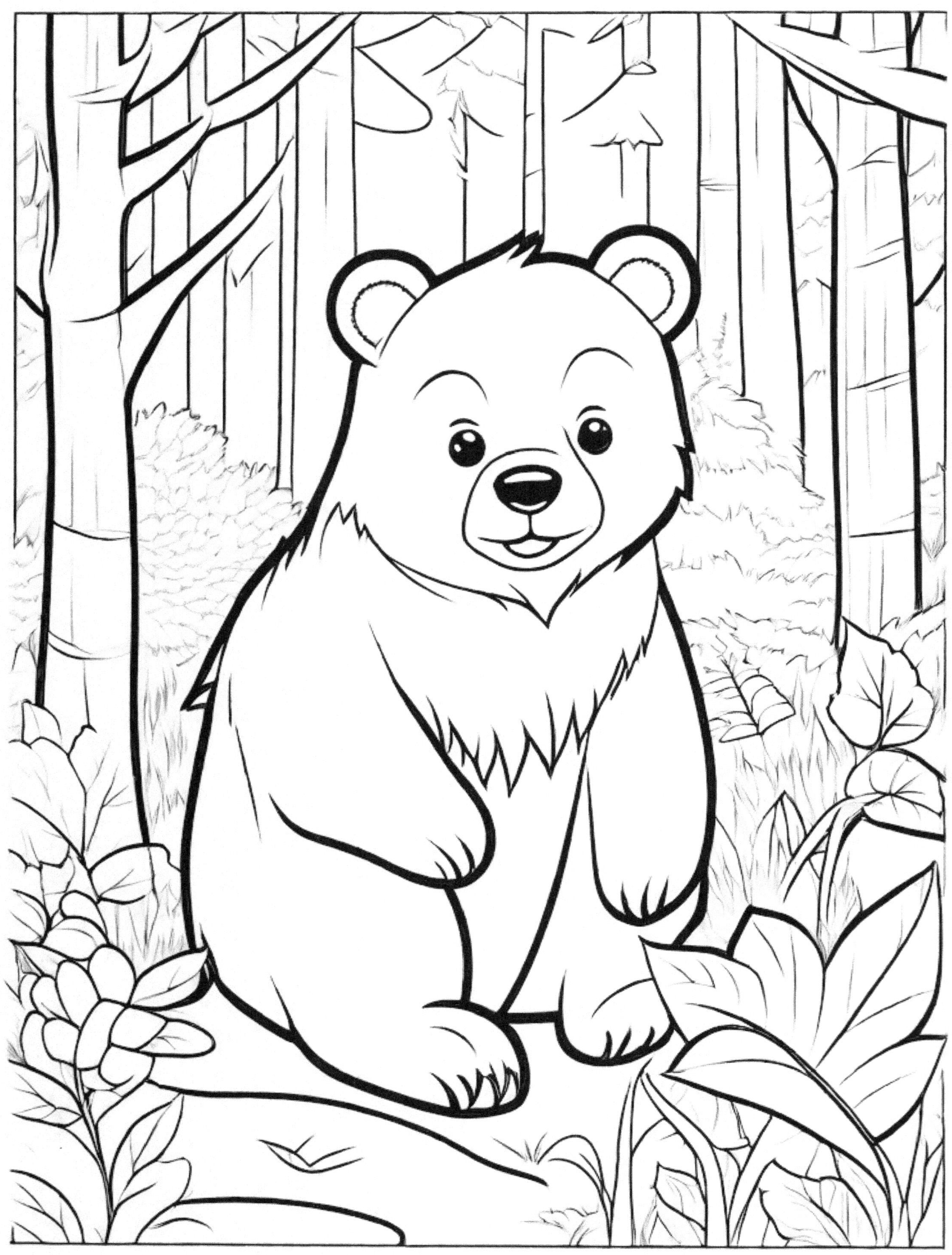

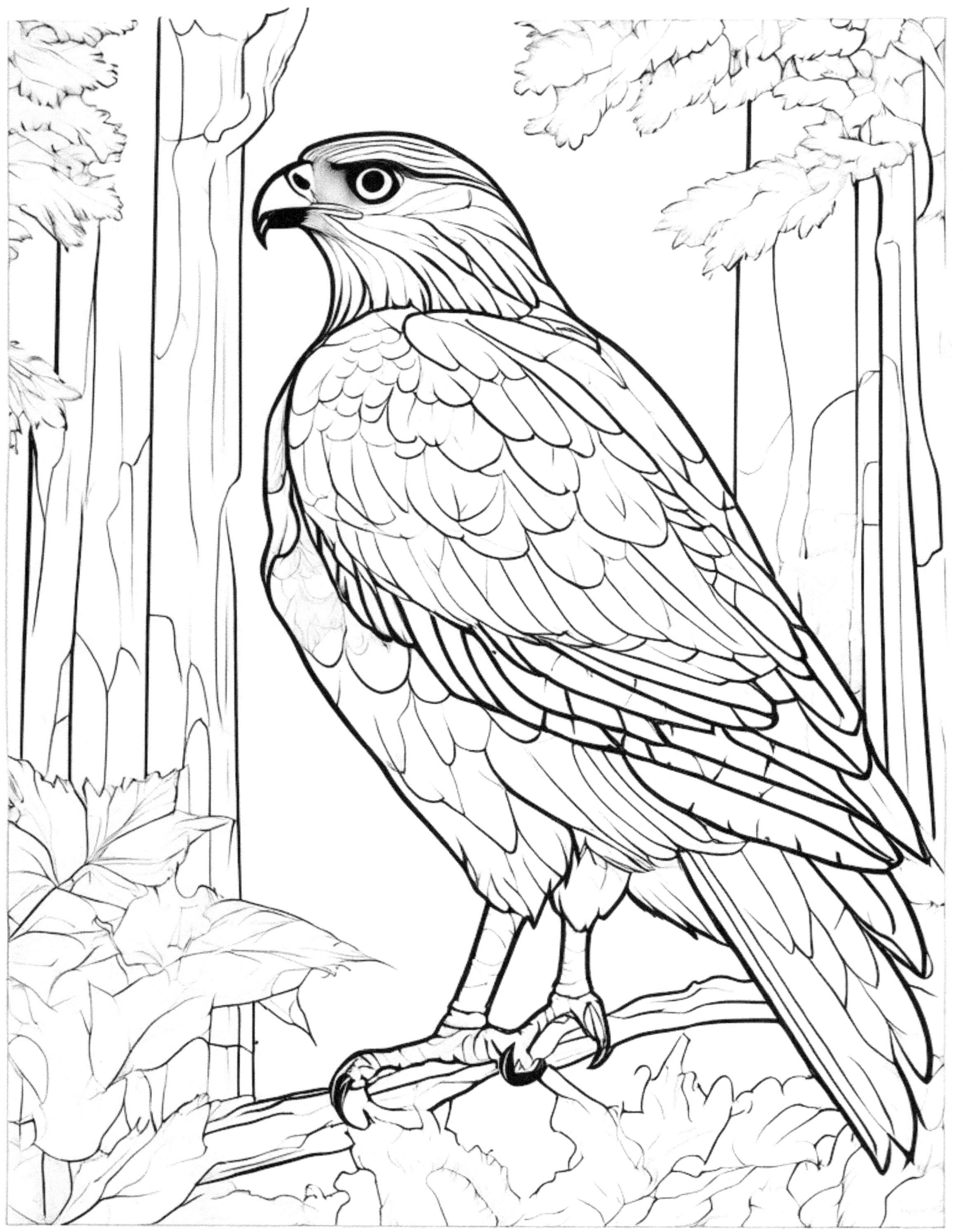

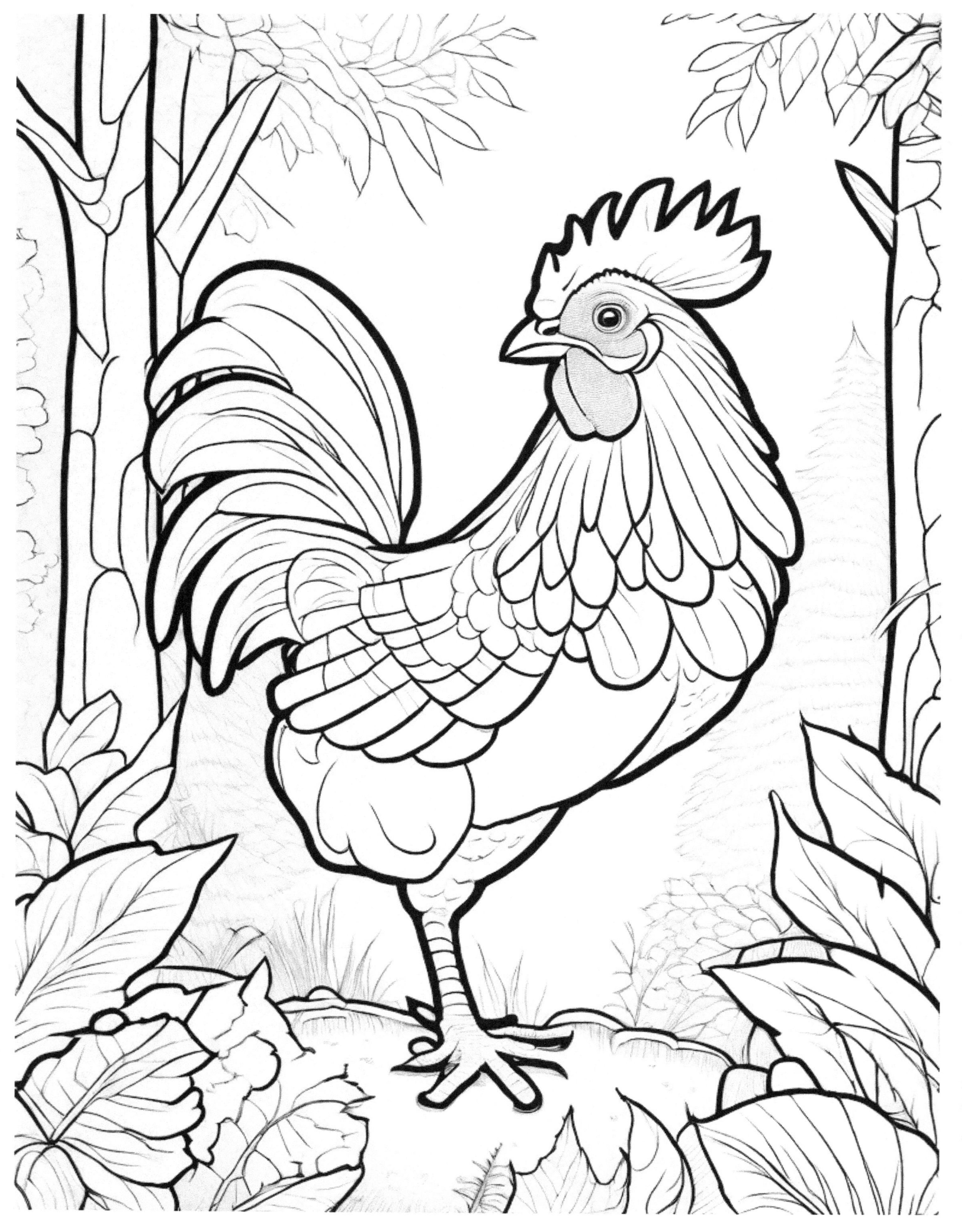

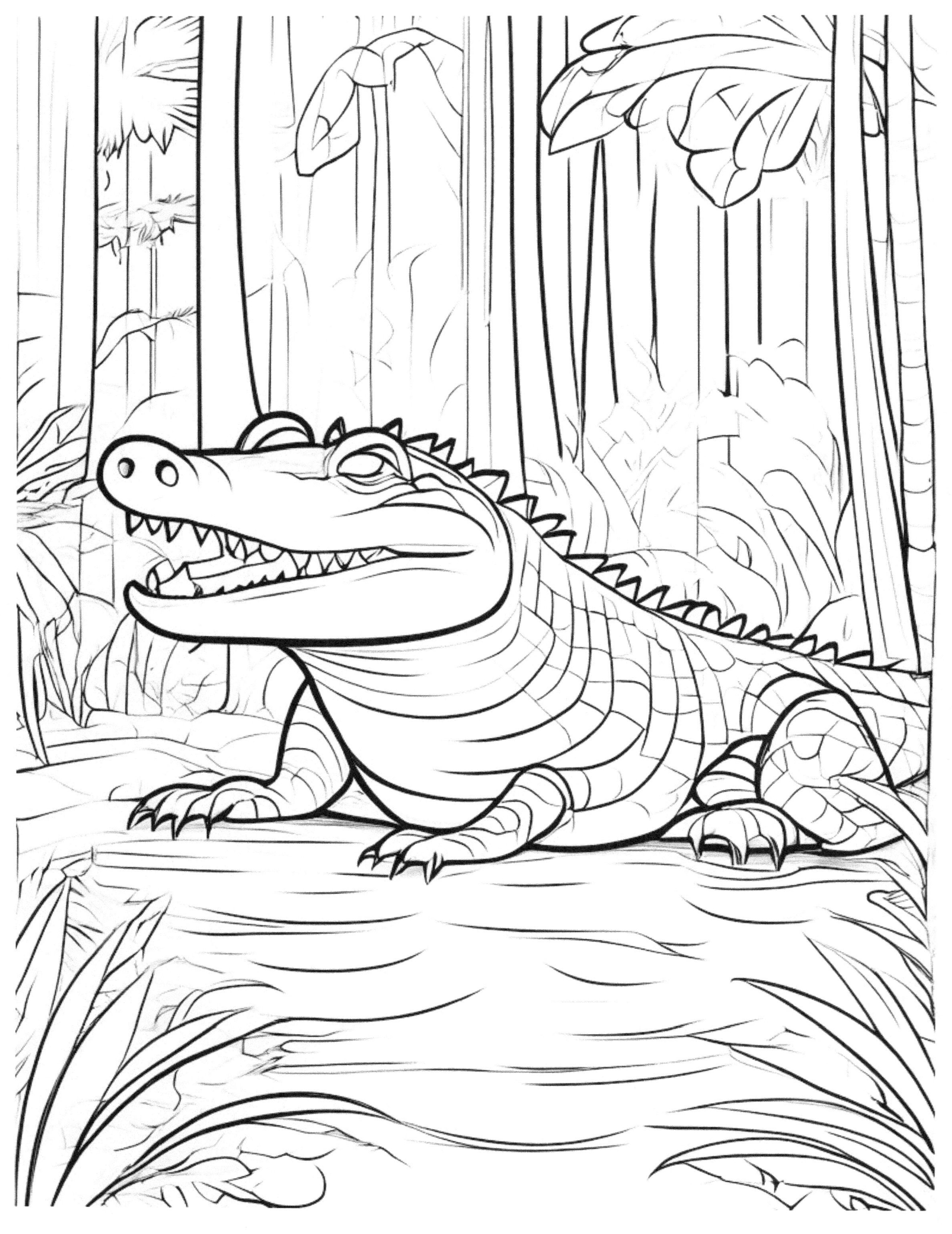

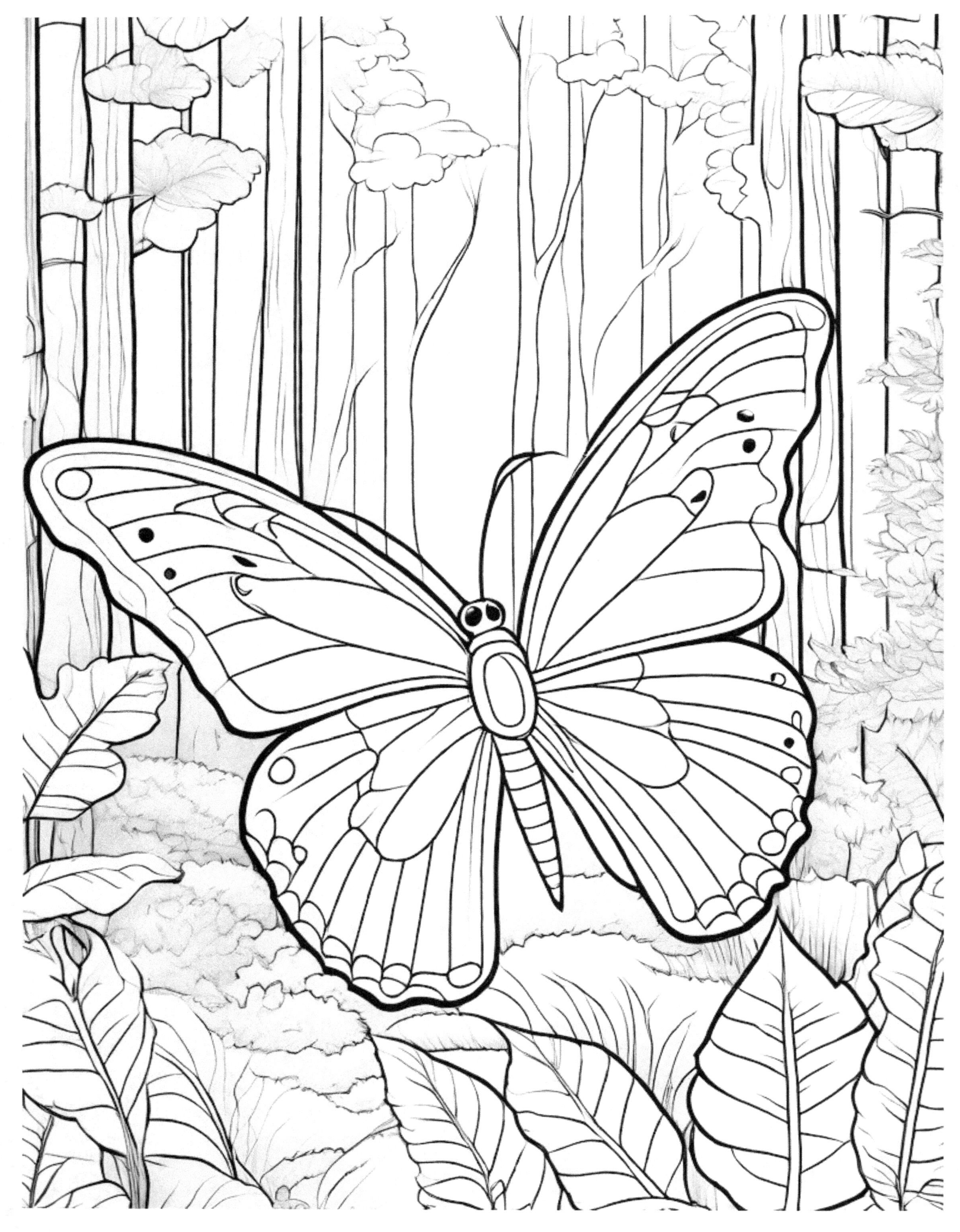

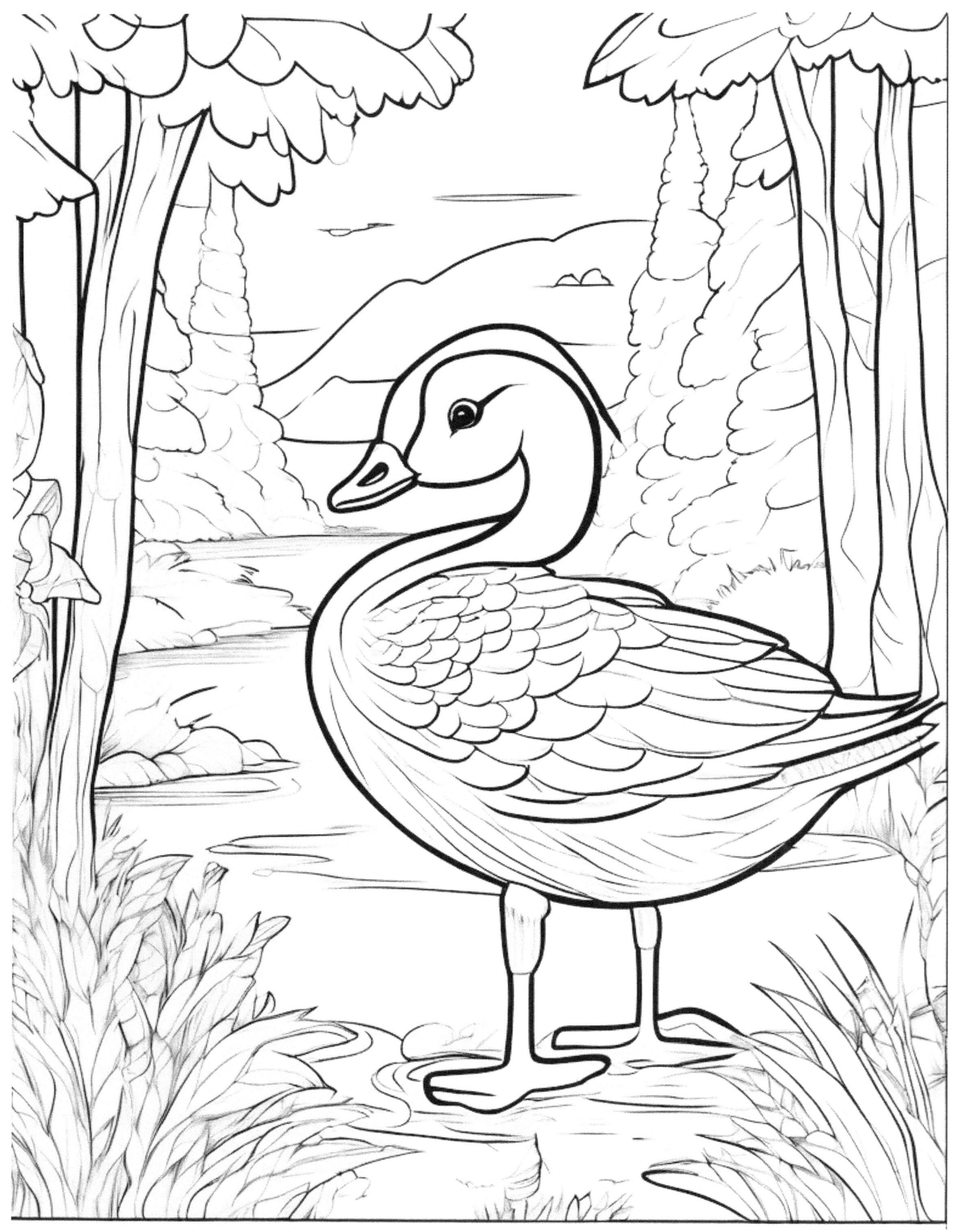

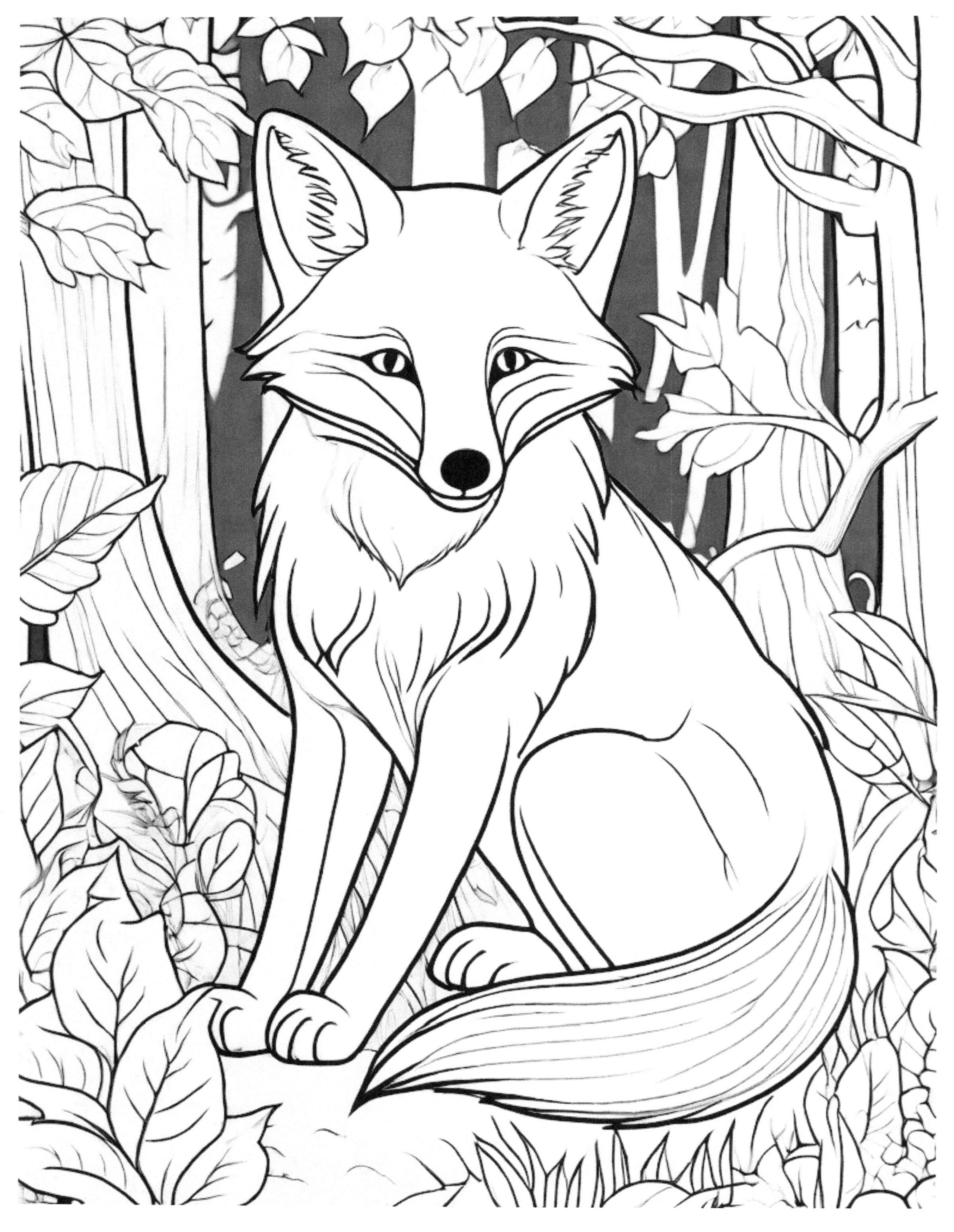

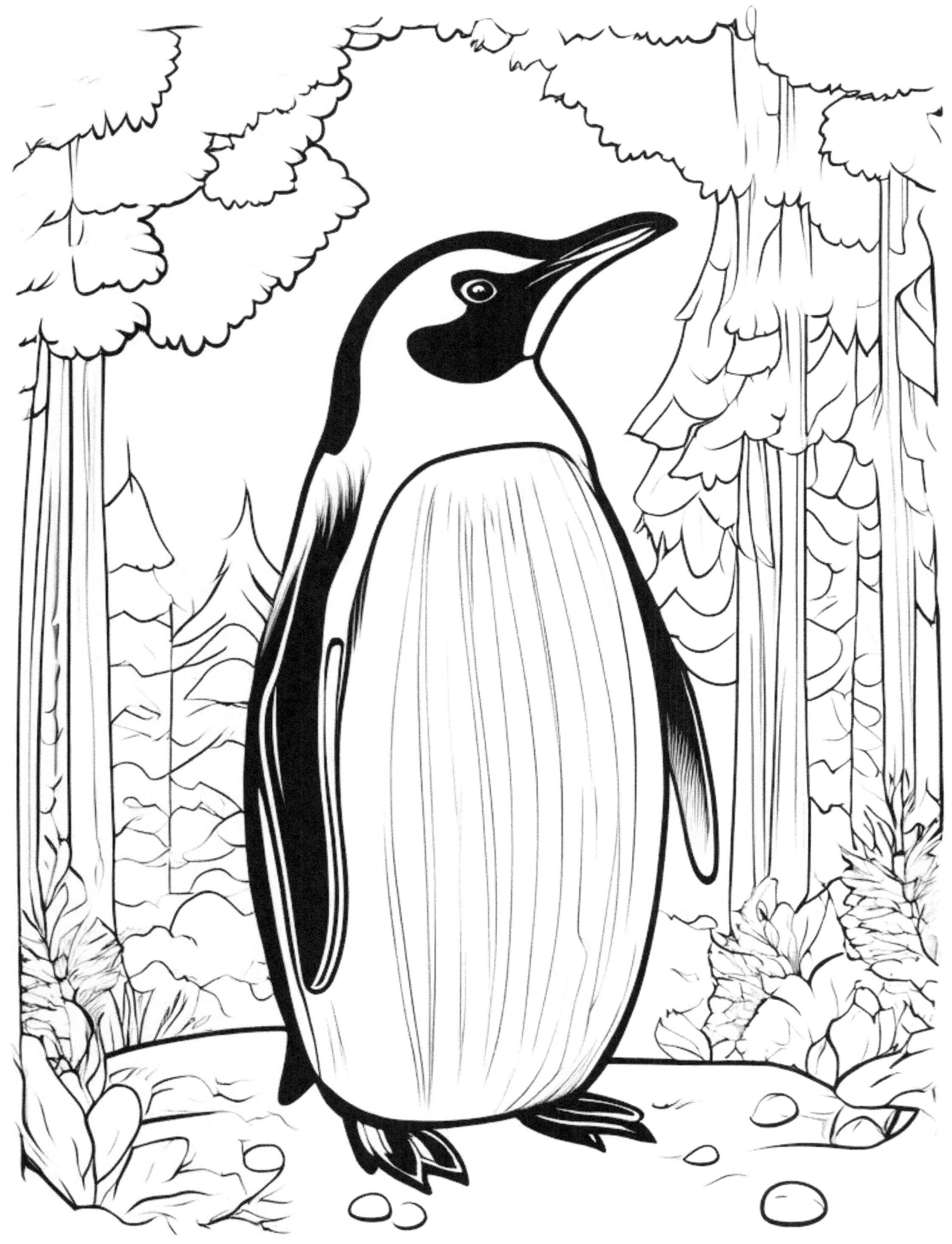

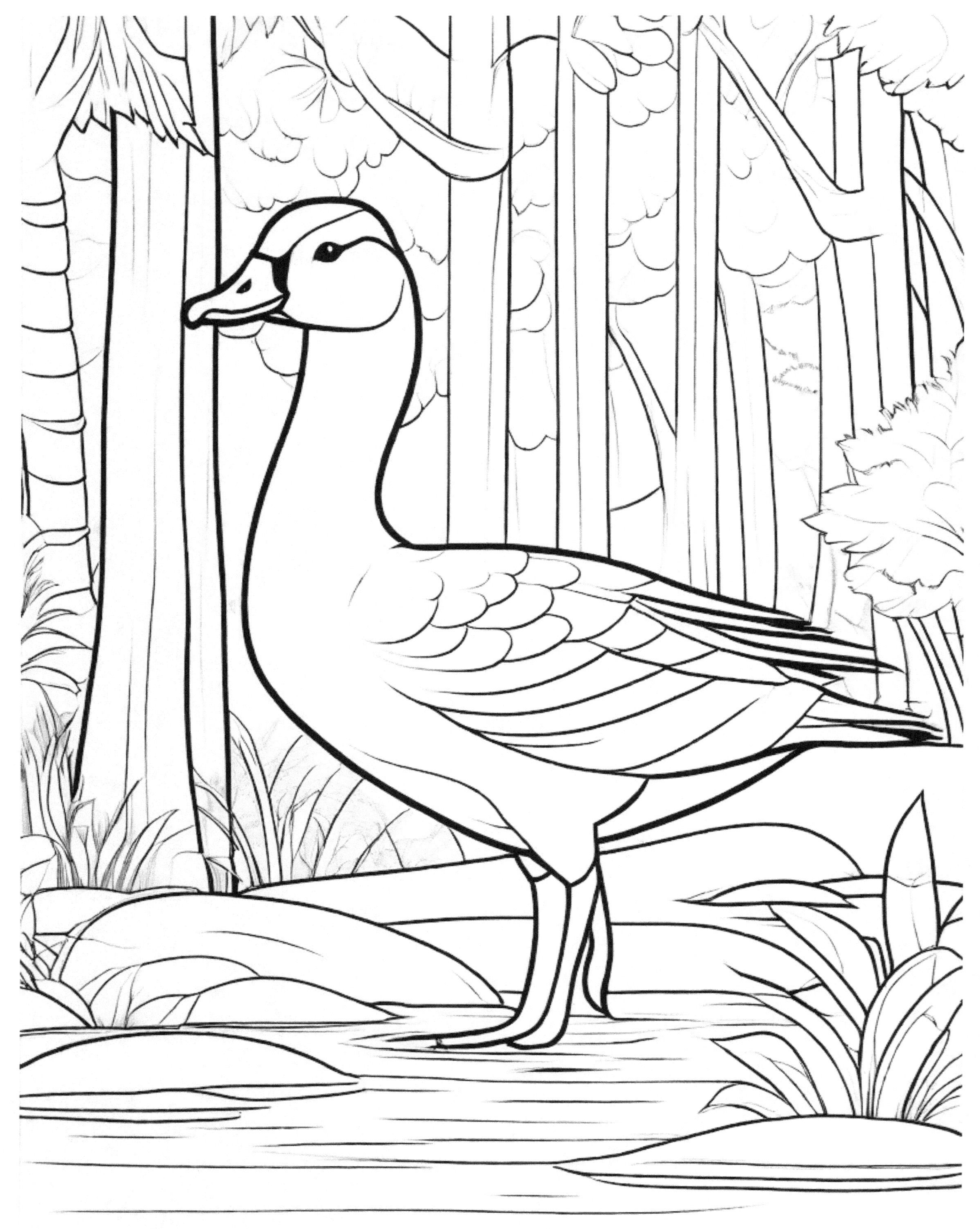

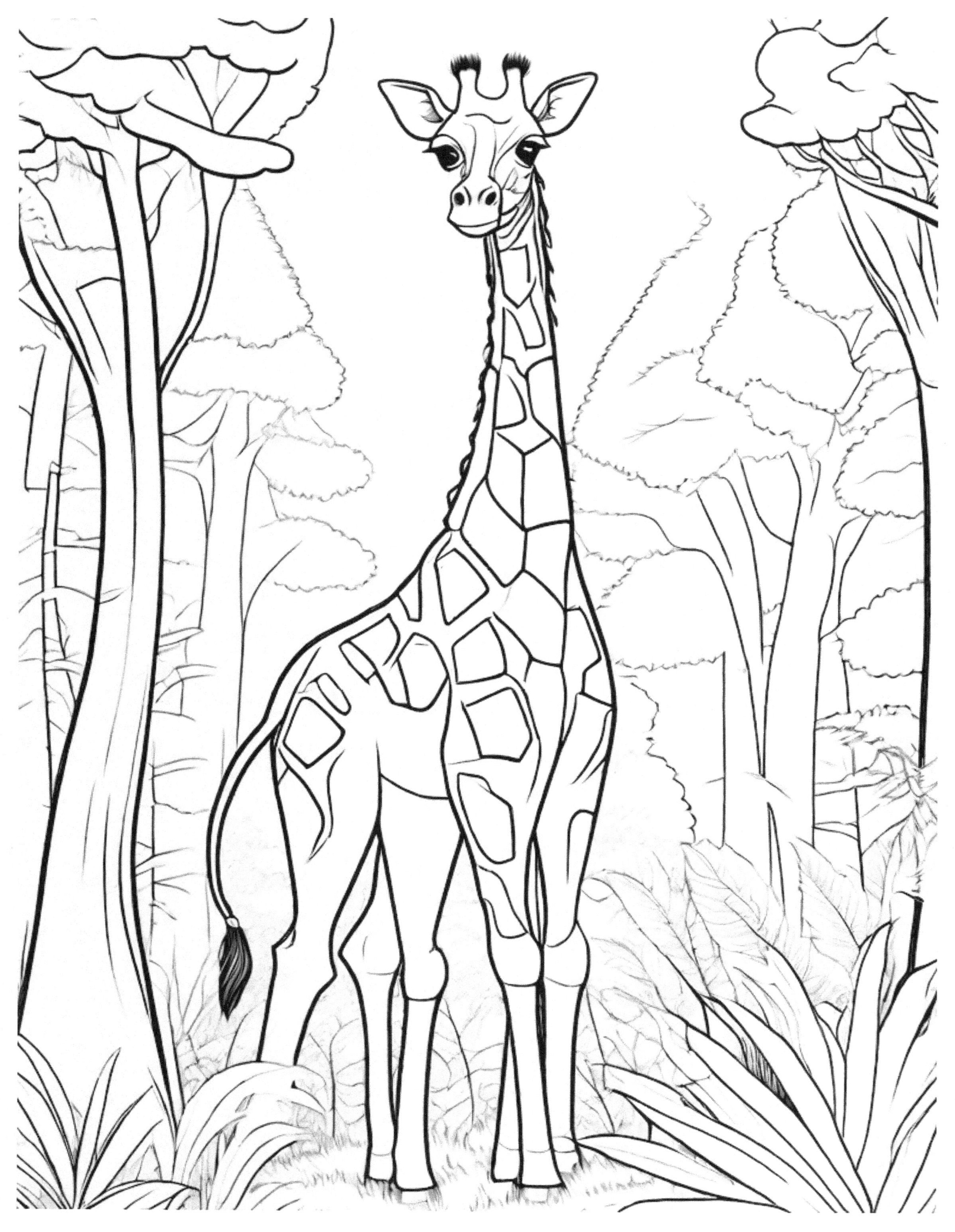

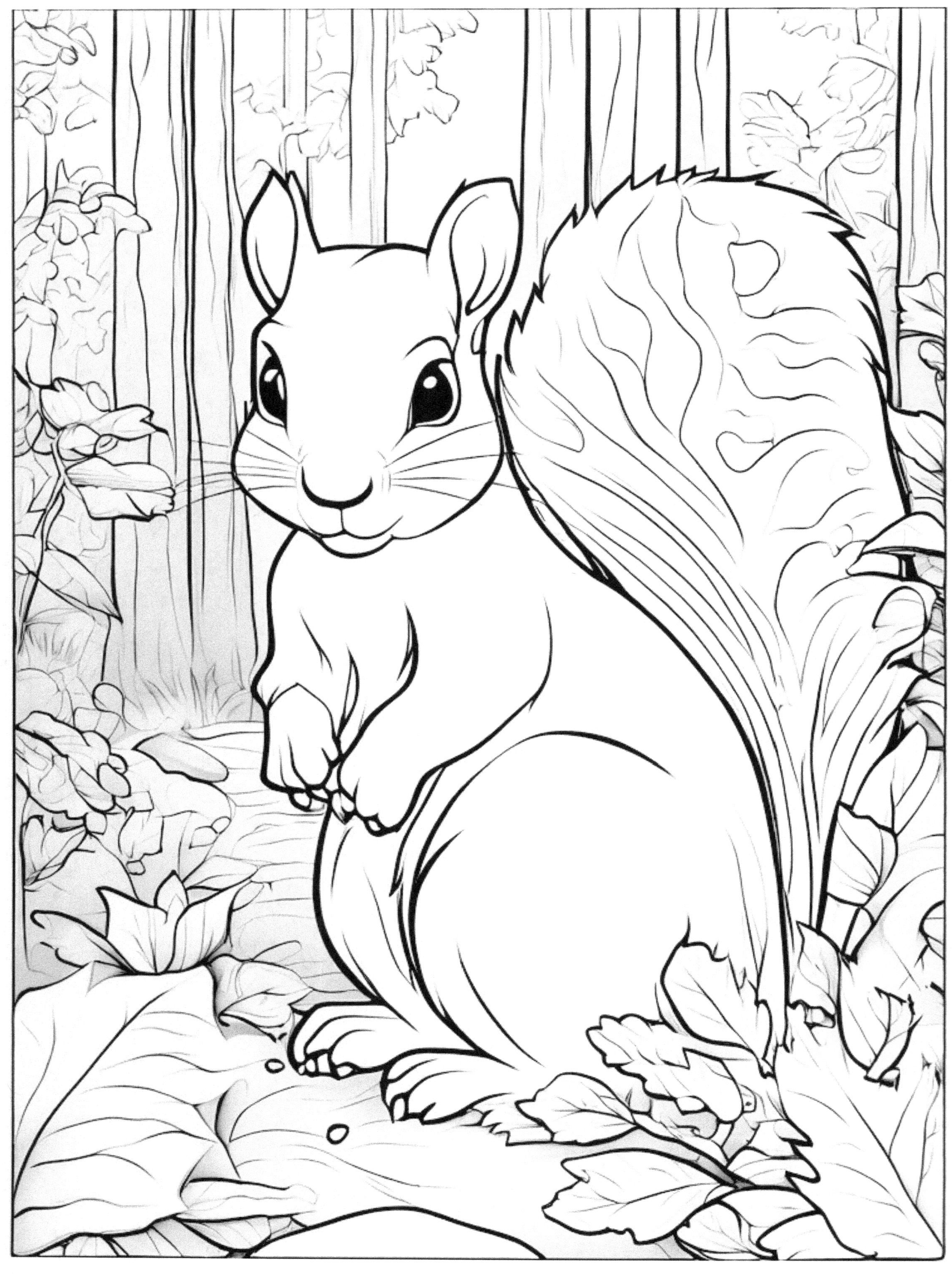

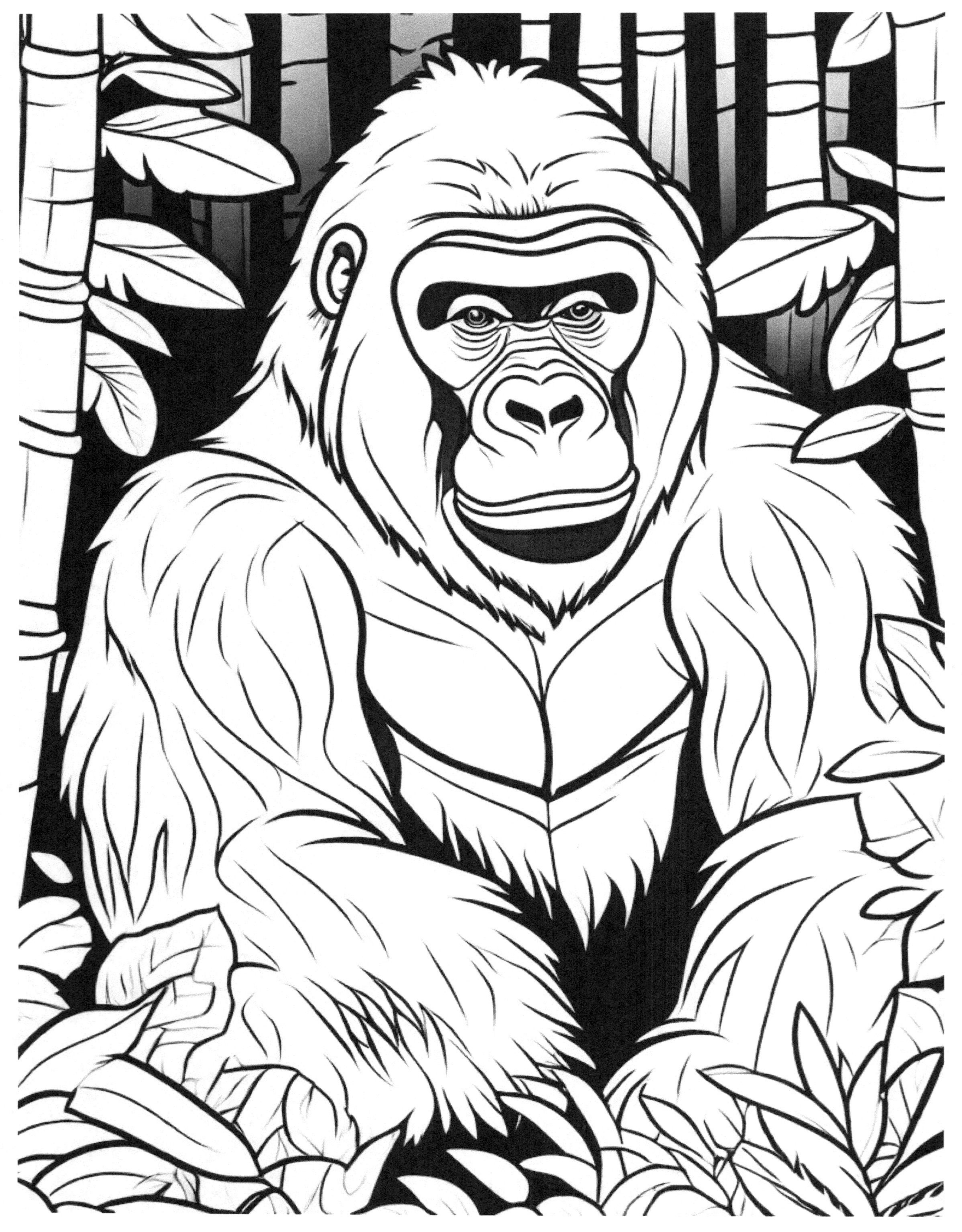

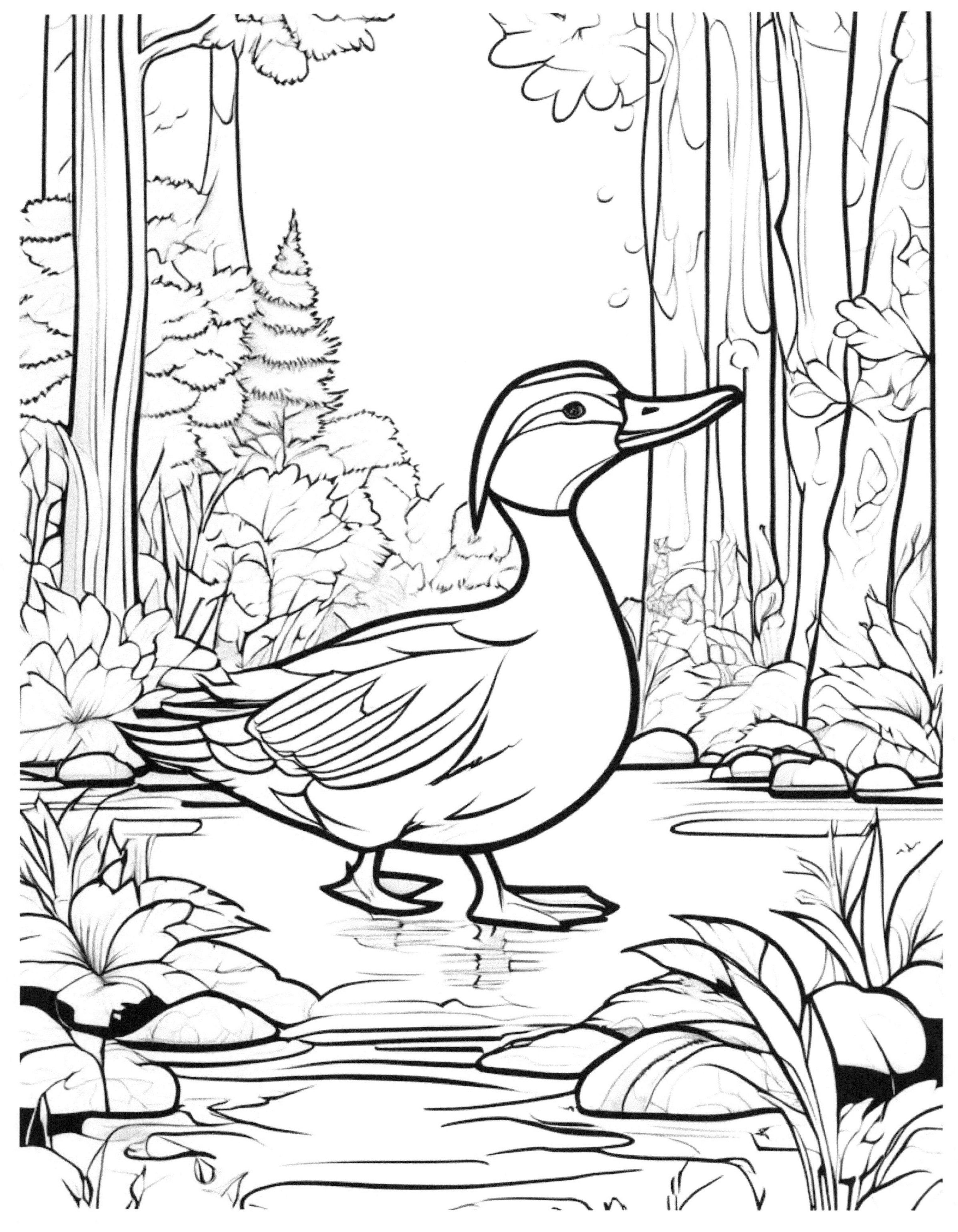

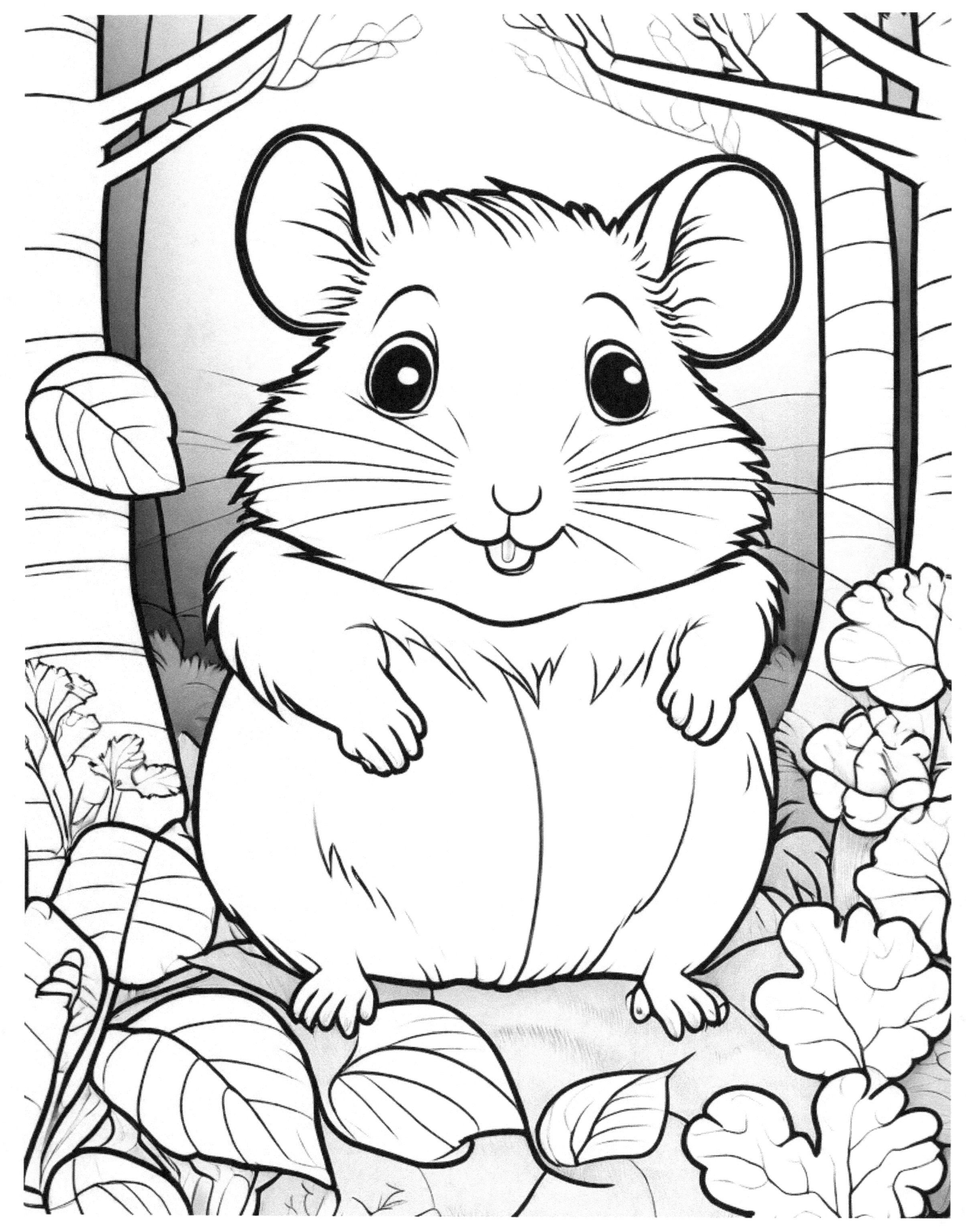

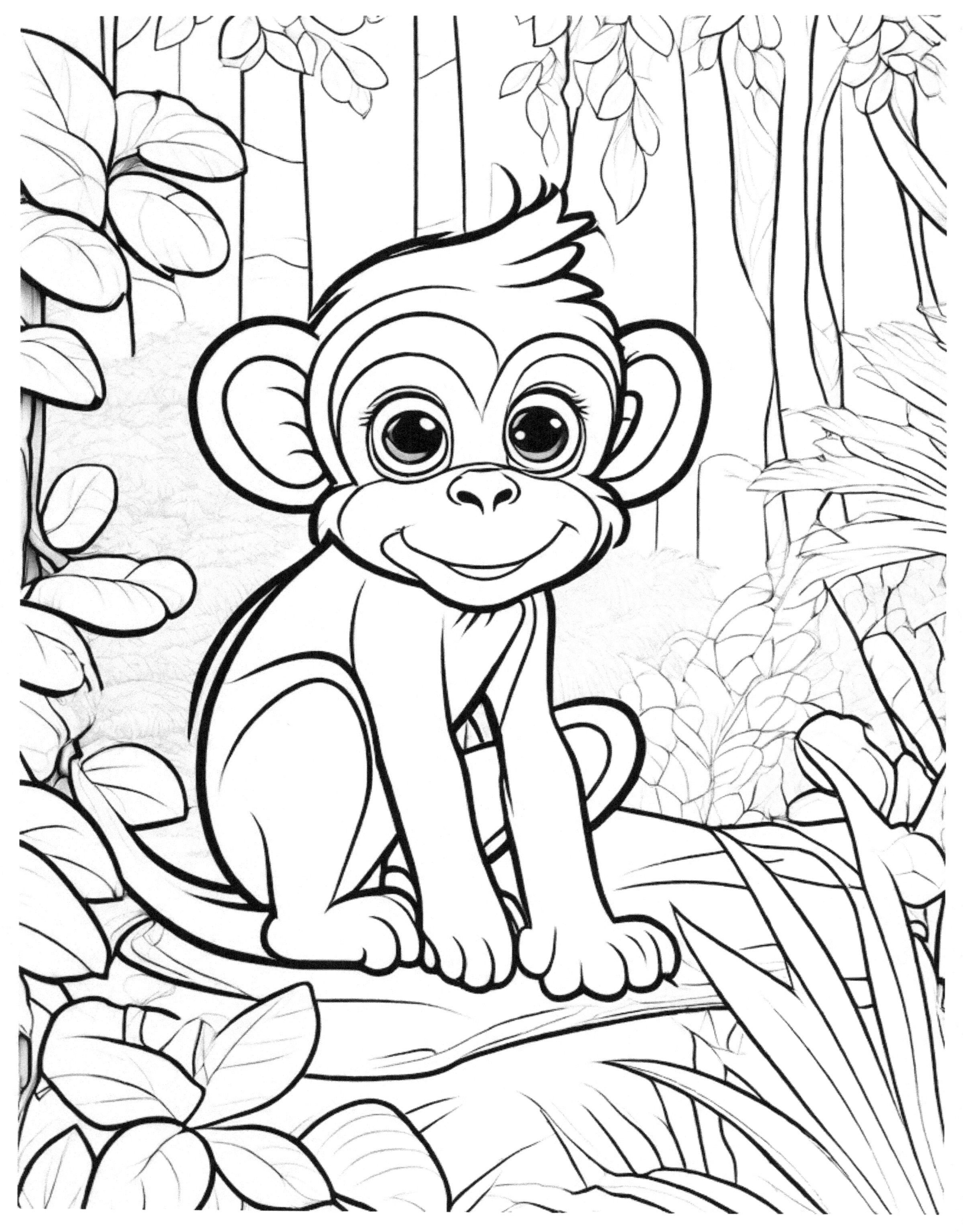

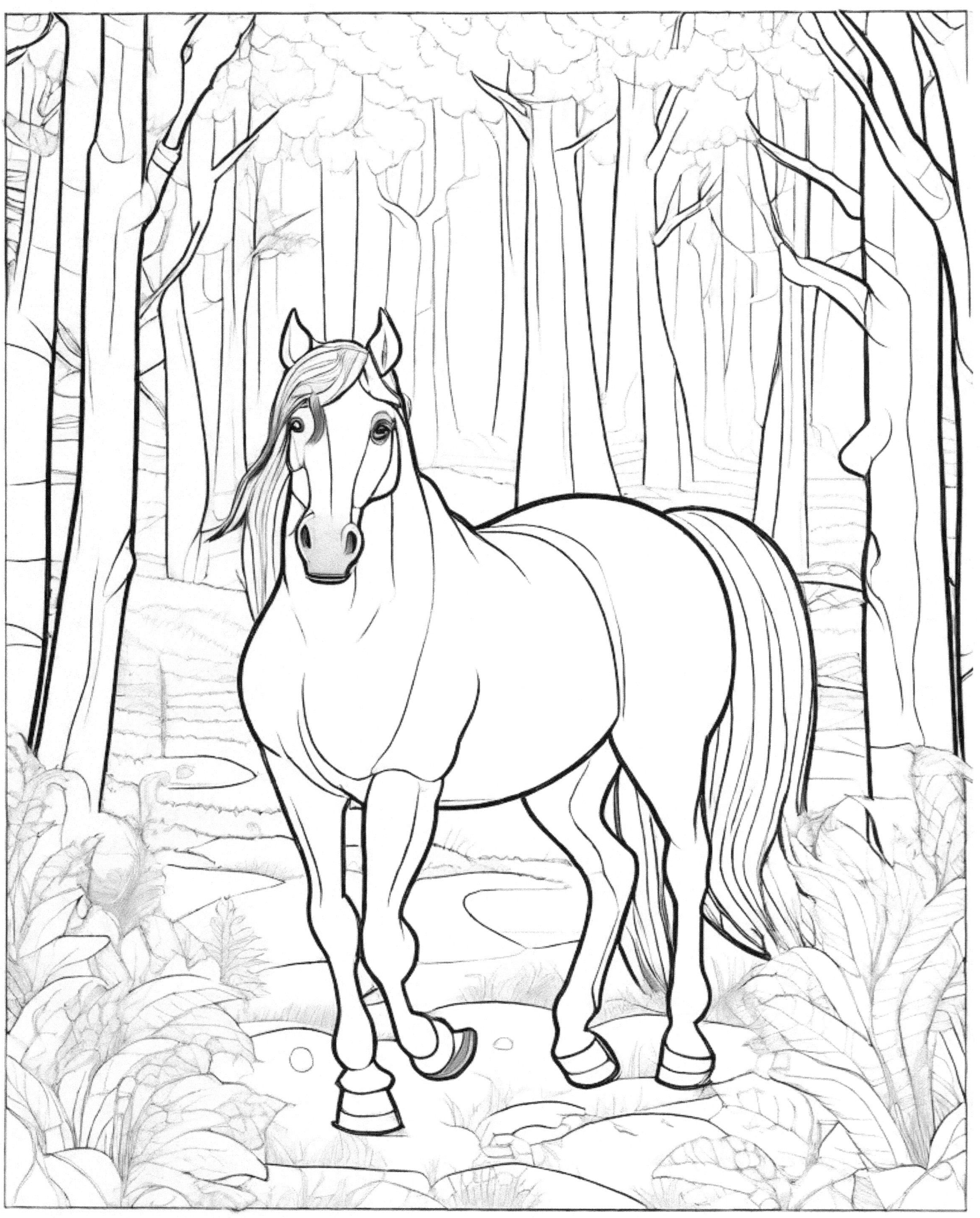

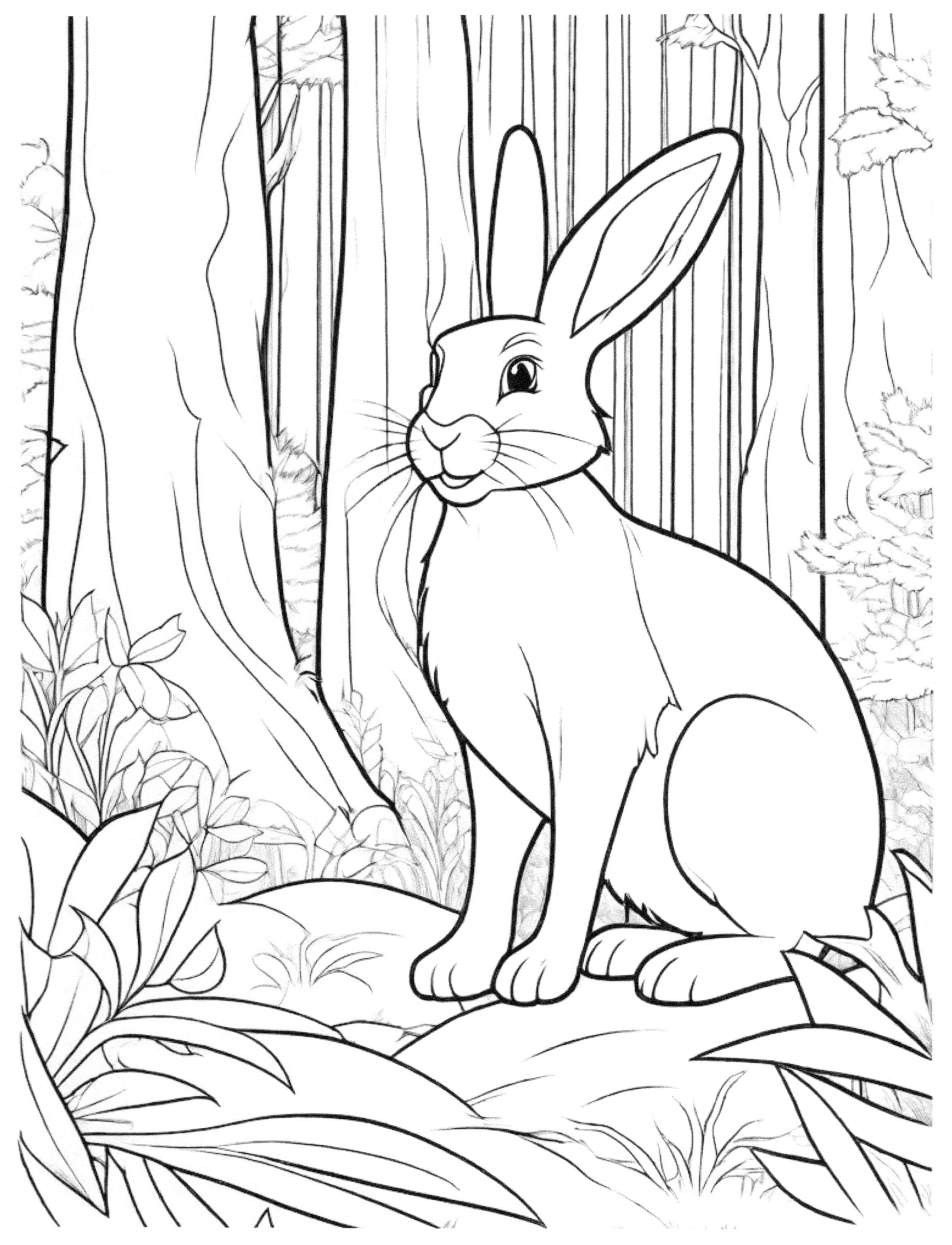

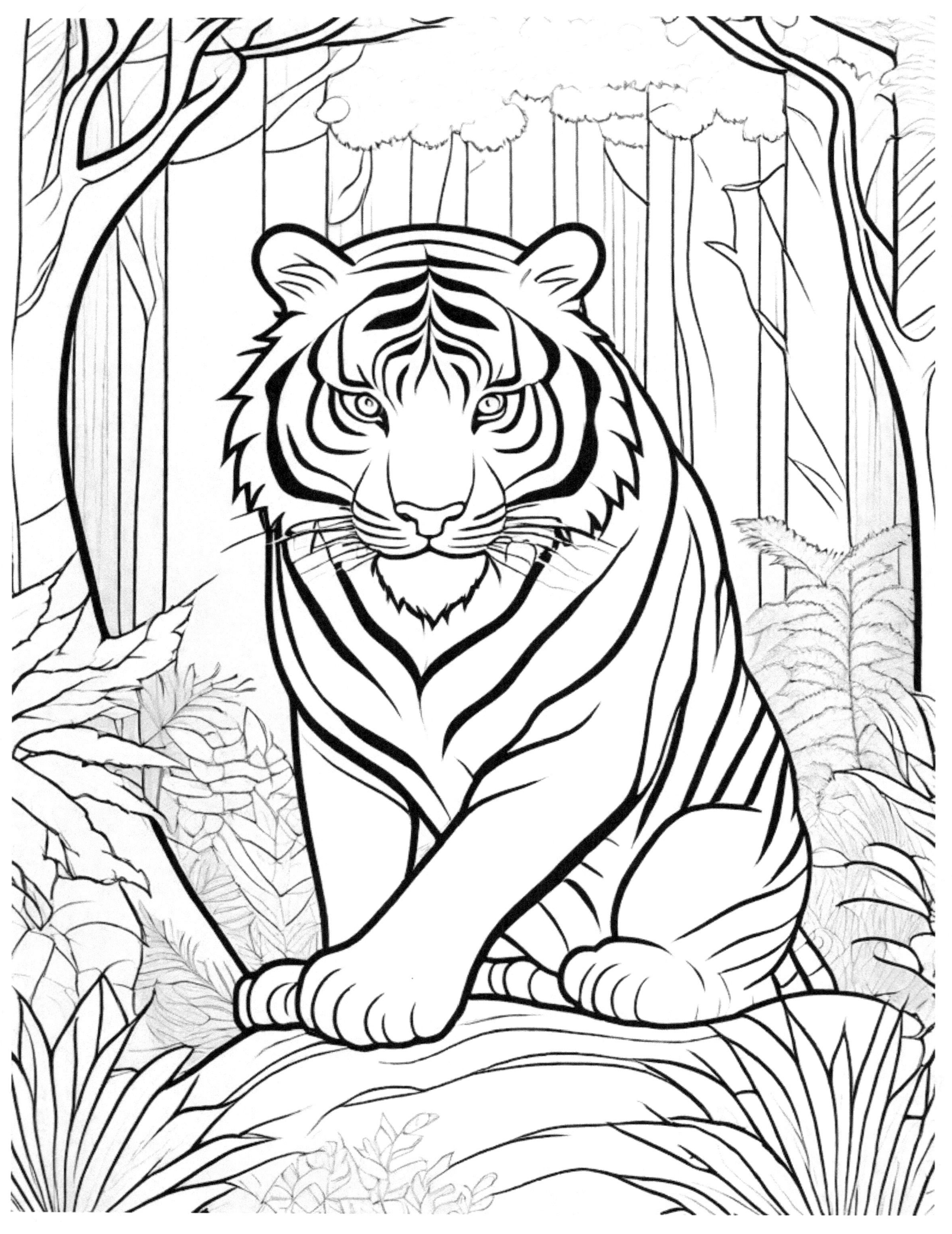

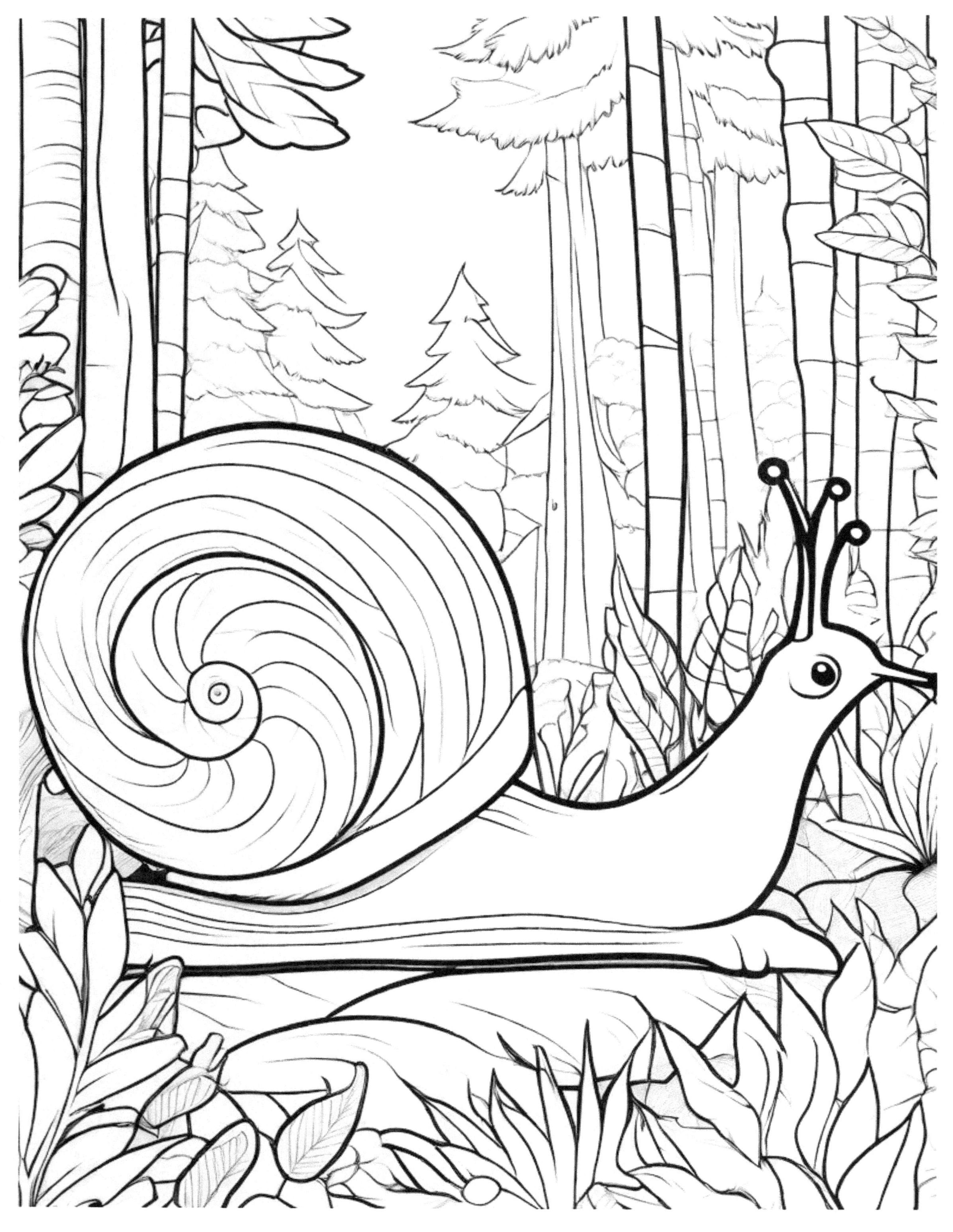

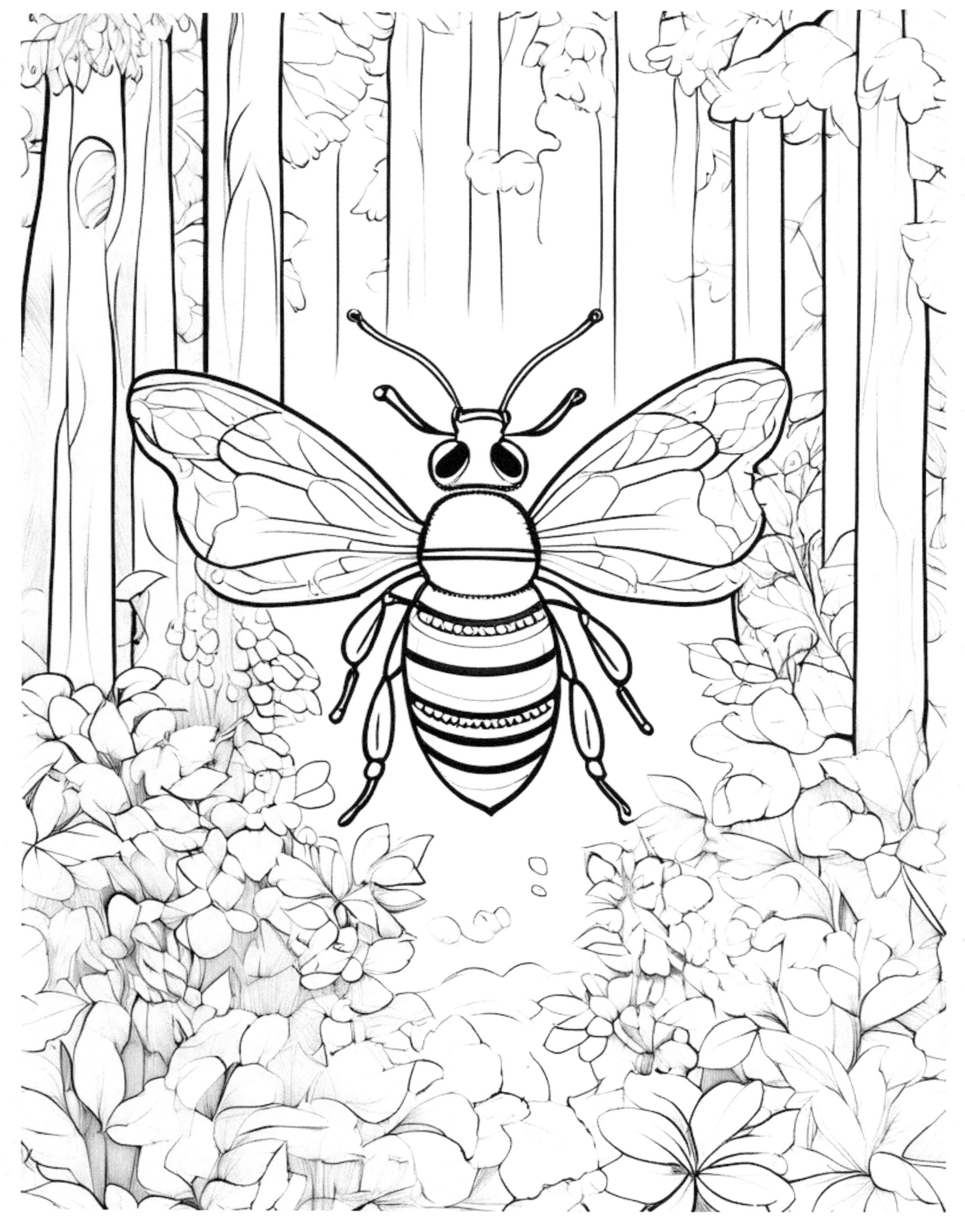

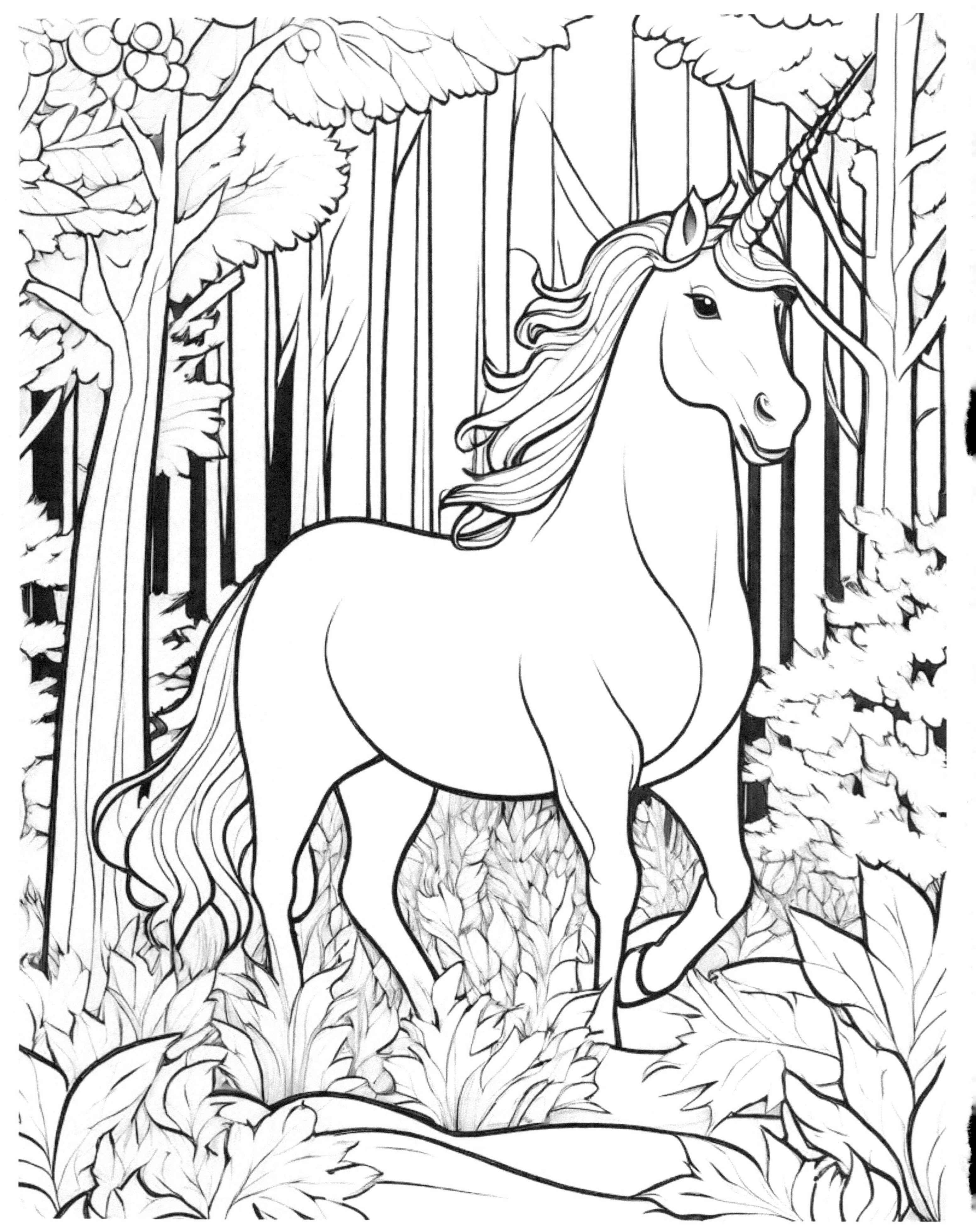